George Lippard

Twayne's United States Authors Series

Lewis Leary, Editor

University of North Carolina, Chapel Hill

TUSAS 417

George Lippard
(1822–1854)
Photograph courtesy of
The Historical Society
of Pennsylvania

George Lippard

By David S. Reynolds

Northwestern University

Twayne Publishers • Boston

George Lippard

David S. Reynolds

Copyright © 1982 by G. K. Hall & Company
All Rights Reserved
Published by Twayne Publishers
A Division of G. K. Hall & Company
70 Lincoln Street
Boston, Massachusetts 02111

Book production by Marne B. Sultz
Book design by Barbara Anderson

Printed on permanent/durable acid-free
paper and bound in The United States
of America.

ʎ
Library of Congress Cataloging in Publication Data

Reynolds, Davis S., 1948–
   George Lippard.

   (Twayne's United States authors series : TUSAS 417)
   Bibliography: p. 132
   Includes index.
   1. Lippard, George, 1822–1854—Criticism and inter-
pretation.   I. Title.   II. Series.
PS2246.L8Z86   813'.3   82-6051
ISBN O-8057-7350-9   AACR2

To Pamela

Contents

About the Author

David S. Reynolds is a literary critic, cultural historian, and college English professor who was born and raised in Rhode Island. After receiving the bachelor's degree in 1970 from Amherst College, he studied American literature at the University of California, Berkeley, where he received the doctorate in 1979. Since 1980 he has been a member of the English department of Northwestern University, where he teaches literature and American Studies.

Mr. Reynolds is the author of *Faith in Fiction: The Emergence of Religious Literature in America* (Harvard University Press, 1981), a study of some 250 eighteenth- and nineteenth-century writers in terms of mainstream religious and literary history. He is also a contributor to the *American Quarterly,* the *New England Quarterly,* the *Journal of American History,* and the *Journal of Popular Culture.* Currently he is working on an anthology of George Lippard's writings, as well as a book comparing major and popular writers of the American Renaissance.

Preface

George Lippard (1822–1854) is an intriguing figure in American literary and cultural history. In his brief life this fiery Philadelphian became widely known as a novelist, social reformer, lecturer, journalist, and newspaper editor. His lurid fictional exposé of Philadelphia's elite classes, *The Quaker City; or, The Monks of Monk Hall* (1844–45), reportedly sold more than 60,000 copies in its first year of publication, went through some twenty-seven American editions and several foreign ones before 1850, and was still selling 30,000 copies annually in the year of Lippard's death. It was the best-selling American novel before the appearance of *Uncle Tom's Cabin* (1852) and was almost as controversial as Harriet Beecher Stowe's novel, becoming, as Lippard boasted in 1849, "more attacked, and more read, than any work of American fiction ever published." "The Quaker City," a phrase Lippard had used ironically, was rapidly adopted as the reverential nickname of Philadelphia. Lippard's sensational fiction earned him notoriety as "the American Eugene Sue," and his unconventional life-style—which included unfashionably long hair and singular dress, well-publicized squabbles with critics and plagiarists, and a wedding ceremony by a moonlit creek—enhanced his image as an eccentric and even immoral writer. At the same time, his jingoistic "legends" of American history were widely admired and sometimes accepted as fact: for instance, his story of the ringing of the Liberty Bell on July 4, 1776, became a national folk myth that found its way into several respectable histories. An outspoken defender of the poor against their capitalist oppressors, Lippard put his reformist theories into practice by founding the Brotherhood of the Union (later renamed the Brotherhood of America), a nationwide labor organization that influenced the founding of the powerful Knights of Labor and that is still alive today.

Lippard was an innovative fictionist with broad popular appeal in a time when American mass culture as we know it today was beginning to emerge. From several tested literary modes Lippard forged new best-selling formulae that pointed toward such later genres as the city novel, muckraking fiction, the gangster story, biblical and Social Gospel fiction, and modern fiction of the grotesque and surreal.

Despite the fact that Lippard is beginning to be taken seriously and that several of his novels have been reprinted since 1968, no comprehensive account of his life and fiction has been published, and he remains a strange ghost figure flitting in and out of what we read about more established American writers. A few recent scholars, retrieving Lippard from nearly a century of critical neglect or condescension, have begun to see richness and complexity where previous appraisers had seen only chaos and peculiarity. In the small amount of criticism devoted to him, Lippard has been placed—either as a descendant, a like-minded contemporary, or a forerunner—among a tantalizing array of well-known authors: Cotton Mather, Jonathan Edwards, Brockden Brown, Cooper, Poe, Hawthorne, Melville, Whitman, Stephen Crane, Theodore Dreiser, Jack London, James T. Farrell, John Dos Passos, and Norman Mailer. Many of the connections drawn between Lippard and these writers have been undeveloped, and in some cases are specious or irresponsible. Yet the wide variety of such connections not only attests to the fertility of Lippard's imagination and the eclecticism of his interests but also underscores the need for a critical revaluation of this vibrant antebellum writer and reformer, who is still dangerously close to becoming a lost figure in our national literature.

David S. Reynolds

Northwestern University

Acknowledgments

I am deeply indebted to the late Roger Butterfield, a journalist and historian with a long-standing interest in George Lippard who patiently answered many questions, supplied me with numerous rare documents relating to Lippard's life, and gave an early draft of this book a careful and constructive reading. I would also like to thank Henry Nash Smith and Richard Bridgman for their encouragement and advice, and especially for their helpful comments on my manuscript.

I have been greatly aided by the staffs of the following organizations: the Historical Society of Pennsylvania and the Library Company; the Free Library in Philadelphia; the Bucks County Historical Society; the New York Public Library; and the Doe Library at the University of California, Berkeley. A travel grant from the American Philosophical Society made possible a research trip to Pennsylvania and New York that was most productive.

Others who have helped me in various ways are Garry Wills, Harrison Hayford, Franklin Rosemont, Mark Lause, Gus and Nancy Ballard, Mimi and Barry Alperin, Margaret Butterfield, Mary and Gordon Pomfrey, and Paul and Peggy Reynolds.

I especially thank Pamela Minkler, who cheerfully adapted to my scholarly schedule and constantly stimulated my thoughts.

Chronology

1822   George Lippard, the fourth of Daniel and Jemima Lippard's six children, born April 10, 1822, on his father's farm in West Nantmeal township, Chester County, Pennsylvania.

1824   Family moves to old Lippard homestead in Germantown, Pennsylvania. Shortly thereafter his parents move to Philadelphia, leaving him and his sisters in Germantown in the care of Aunts Catherine and Mary and grandfather Michael Lippard.

ca. 1829–1832   Attends old Concord School in Germantown.

1831   His mother dies after giving birth to a son who dies in infancy.

1832   Aunts sell the Germantown homestead and take him and his sisters to live in Philadelphia apart from their father, who marries a second time in 1833.

1837   Joins Western M. E. Church in Philadelphia. Attends Catherine Livingston Garretson's Classical School in Rhinebeck, New York, with the aim of studying for the Methodist ministry. Disillusioned, he returns to Philadelphia, where he witnesses his father's death on October 27.

1838–1841   Works as legal assistant for attorney William Badger and then for Attorney-General Ovid F. Johnson.

1840   Begins writing *The Ladye Annabel*.

1841   Quits law, is introduced to John S. DuSolle, editor of a Philadelphia newspaper, the *Spirit of the Times*.

1842   Works for the *Spirit of the Times* until April 9, publishing in the newspaper the "Our Talisman" series, the Billy Brier police-court reports, "The Sanguine Poetaster," "The Bread Crust Papers," reports of Charles Dickens's visit to America, two Oriental allegories, and numerous local news stories. His story "Philippe de Agramont" published July 9 in the *Saturday Evening Post*, which publishes serially his first novel, *Herbert Tracy*, October 22 through November 26.

1843   Joins staff of a Philadelphia weekly, the *Citizen Soldier*. Becomes the newspaper's main writer and by July its chief editor. Publishes in the paper several legends of the American Revolution, two medieval Gothic narratives ("Adrian the Neophyte" and *The Ladye Annabel*), various political essays and news briefs, and literary criticism, including ardent defenses of his friend Edgar Allan Poe as well as the satirical columns "The Spermaceti Papers" and "The Walnut Coffin Papers."

1844   Publishes *The Ladye Annabel* and *Herbert Tracy* in book form, the latter volume containing a letter sent to him by Poe evaluating *The Ladye Annabel*. In fall publishes first serial segments of *The Quaker City; or, The Monks of Monk Hall*. Proposed play of *The Quaker City* nearly causes riot outside Chesnut Street Theater.

1845   After remaining segments of *The Quaker City* appear, all segments are gathered together and published as single volume in May. Sales boom; new editions follow. December 8 gives first historical lecture at the William Wirt Institute, Philadelphia.

1846   Famous Liberty Bell legend printed January 3 in Philadelphia *Saturday Courier,* which on July 4 begins printing his series of sixty-two Revolutionary legends that runs through December 23, 1848. *Blanche of Brandywine* and the unfinished *Nazarene* published. Begins lecturing widely.

1847   March 5 through 20, campaigns for post of District Commissioner of Philadelphia, losing a close election. May 15 marries Rose Newman by moonlight on rock above Wissahickon Creek. Publishes *The Rose of Wissahikon, Washington and His Generals,* and *Legends of Mexico.*

1848   Publishes several short pieces, including tribute to Charles Brockden Brown, in Charles Chauncey Burr's new quarterly, the *Nineteenth Century.* Daughter Mima born March 31. Publishes *'Bel of Prairie Eden* and *Paul Ardenheim.* In July addresses National Reform Congress and in fall campaigns for presidential candidate Zachary Taylor. Sister Harriet dies December 28. On December 30 he publishes first issue of his weekly newspaper the *Quaker City,* which he edits until June 1850.

1849   In the *Quaker City* weekly he publishes many reformist essays and five new serial novels: *Memoirs of a Preacher, The Man with the Mask, The Entranced, The Empire City,* and *The Killers.* Visited July 12 by the impoverished Poe, whom he aids by collecting money from literary associates. Founds labor organization, the Brotherhood of the Union, which grows rapidly. Publishes moving eulogy of Poe. Daughter Mima dies late October.

1850   Publishes *Washington and His Men.* In the *Quaker City* weekly publishes essays defending Poe and the feminist Lucretia Mott. Helps found Philadelphia tailoresses' cooperative in March. Son Paul born in May. At First Annual Convocation of the Brotherhood, he is elected Supreme Washington for life.

1851–1854 Lectures widely on behalf of the Brotherhood throughout eastern states and as far away as Ohio, Maryland, and Virginia.

1851 Baby son Paul dies March 1. Twenty-six-year-old wife, Rose, dies May 21. Publishes only edition of the *White Banner*, a Brotherhood organ containing *Adonai: The Pilgrim of Eternity*.

1852 Late in year begins brief term as literary editor of the *New York National Democrat*.

1853 Publishes *The Midnight Queen* and *New York: Its Upper Ten and Lower Million*. In June attends the Eighth National Industrial Congress in Wilmington, Delaware, which is presided over by a member of the Brotherhood.

1854 Writes serial story, "Eleanor; or, Slave Catching in the Quaker City," while bedridden with tuberculosis. Dies February 9, 1854, a month before his thirty-second birthday.

1876 In year of America's centennial celebration, three of his patriotic novels about American Revolution (*Washington and His Generals, Paul Ardenheim, Blanche of Brandywine*) and his most famous urban novel, *The Quaker City*, are reprinted by T. B. Peterson and Brothers.

1885 Large monument erected to his memory in Odd Fellows Cemetery, Philadelphia.

1900 His Brotherhood (now the Brotherhood of America) consists of 21,278 members among 233 circles and homes. At annual convocation in October, Brotherhood members make mass pilgrimage to his grave, singing hymns and giving speeches in his honor.

1922   The Brotherhood celebrates centennial of his birth in April with another pilgrimage to his grave.

1969–1971   Five of his novels *(The Quaker City, Blanche of Brandywine, Washington and His Generals, The Empire City,* and *New York: Its Upper Ten and Lower Million)* are reprinted in America, one (a translation of *The Quaker City)* in Germany.

1980   The Brotherhood consists of some 200 members and operates as small insurance group in Pennsylvania and New Jersey.

Chapter One

An Eventful Life

In 1841 the nineteen-year-old George Lippard, a shabbily dressed youth with few prospects for success after his abandonment of careers in the ministry and the law, was wandering the streets of Philadelphia and spending nights in abandoned houses or vacant artist studios. Four years later Lippard had become the city's best-selling novelist and the center of a storm of controversy. His rags had been replaced by a natty blue velvet coat buttoned tightly at his slim waist, with a billowing necktie and black cape adding Byronic flourish to his appearance.

His vitriolic novel about secret corruption among respectable Philadelphians had divided the city. On one hand, Lippard was damned as "a writer of immoral works," his novel as "a disgusting mass of filth." Lippard claimed that he had to arm himself against assassins, and a proposed dramatization of his novel resulted in the gathering of a turbulent mob outside the Chesnut Street Theater that only the entire city police force could prevent from erupting into a riot. At the same time, Lippard's friends were quick to defend him as a new messiah of the poor, a misunderstood genius on the level of Dante or Shakespeare. By the time of his death less than a decade later Lippard had written more than twenty books and innumerable periodical pieces, defended in print his maligned friend Poe, lectured in most of the eastern states, engaged spiritedly in state and national politics, edited his own newspaper for over a year, and founded a secret brotherhood that revered him as the "Supreme Washington."

Lippard's life, one of the most unusual in American letters, is a tale of intense ambition and energy, meteoric fame, colorful controversies, and continual tragedy.

Toward *The Quaker City* (1822–1843)

George Lippard's ancestors were colonial settlers of English and German origin. Two forerunners on his mother's side, Reuben and Nathaniel Ford, were English emigrants to America; their son David was a prosperous farmer in Brandywine Hundred, Delaware, noted for his devout Methodism. On his father's side, Lippard's lineage reached back to John Cook, who had come to the Philadelphia suburb of Germantown to escape religious persecution in his native Germany, and to John Libbert (later changed to Lippard to suit local pronunciation), a German Palatine who arrived in Pennsylvania in 1736 and also settled in Germantown. John Libbert's son Michael became a wheelwright and in 1773 married Catherine, the daughter of John Cook. One of their nine children, Daniel Lippard (George's father), was born in 1790, taught school in Philadelphia for a number of years, and in 1815 married David Ford's daughter Jemima, whom he had met at a ship launching in Kensington. In the year of his marriage Daniel gave up teaching and was elected Treasurer of Philadelphia County, a post he held for three years.

In 1820 Daniel bought a fertile ninety-two-acre farm in West Nantmeal township, Chester County, thirty-seven miles west of Philadelphia. Here George Lippard was born on April 10, 1882, the fourth of Daniel and Jemima's six children. In the fall of 1822 the Nantmeal farm was put up for sale. Two years later, after Daniel had suffered a crippling wagon accident while delivering farm goods to market, the family moved to the old Lippard homestead in Germantown, where George's German-speaking grandfather Michael was still living. By 1825 George's parents, both of whom had become physically incapable of raising a large family, had moved to Philadelphia, leaving George and his sisters in Germantown in the care of their grandfather and their two maiden aunts, Catherine and Mary.

George's six years in Germantown (1825–1831) nurtured several of the anxieties and loyalties that would be revealed in his adult writings. The gloom pervading the Germantown household is suggested by a sampler sewn by Catherine in 1825, which is full of images of sorrow and death. George, a sickly and intense boy who wore his hair long in back-country Pennsylvania-German fashion, was thought to be a "queer" fellow "of no account" by some of his mates at the old Concord School across the road from his home.[1] He liked to play hooky and fish or hunt for birds by the Wissahickon, the lovely, winding creek that would be the setting of several of his romances. The Germantown area was rich in Revolutionary history and in folklore about early Pennsylvania pietists. George's Aunt Mary, who had been born at the start of the Revolution, fanned George's historical curiosity and patriotism by telling him stirring tales of Revolutionary battles and heroes. At the same time, George's religious impulse was quickened by the Methodist preachers who periodically visited the Germantown house, bringing vivid reports of their frontier itinerancies.

Another important feature of the Germantown period was the steady sale of the family property, which had been owned by Lippards since 1784. To keep the family solvent, George's aunts sold first the orchard and garden and finally the house itself to Edward Johnson, a Germantown tanner. In later life George bitterly wondered why "this old house, this bit of land could not have been spared from the land sharper and mortgage hunter," whom George had come to view as the murderous "destroyer of the homestead."[2]

A contemporary biographer of Lippard portrayed him as a Dantesque youth "perpetually haunted by a sense of his own mortality," which is not surprising since between 1830 and 1843 George was to lose his grandfather, his mother, his infant brother, his father, and two of his sisters.[3] Shortly after the death of his mother in 1831, George moved with his aunts and sisters to Philadelphia. George's father, who was running a grocery store and had been elected constable of Philadelphia's South Ward, remarried in 1833. George never went to live with his father and stepmother. While little is known about George's early Philadelphia period, we get the general picture of a frail, feverishly imaginative boy finding refuge from misfortune in religion, in solitary walks out to the country, and in the incessant reading of the Bible, history, and fiction. During this period George was in the habit of conducting religious services in the woods with friends, and at fifteen he was received as a probationary member of the Western M. E. Church in Philadelphia. In August 1837 Cornelia Bayard, a spinster who thought George showed academic promise, persuaded him, against the wishes of his aunts and sisters, to go to Catherine Livingston Garretson's Classical School in Rhinebeck, New York, with the aim of eventually studying for the Methodist ministry at Middletown College.

At Rhinebeck George became quickly disenchanted with the idea of becoming a preacher. The school's hierarchical distinctions between faculty and students conflicted with his concept of Christian equality. The highly sensitive youth became especially upset when the director of the school, the Rev. Samuel Bell, one day failed to offer him a peach from a bagful he had just bought. "If such are the fruits of piety," George is said to have declared, "I will have none of it."[4]

George's return to Philadelphia brought more disappointment. He witnessed his father's death on October 27, 1837, then learned that he was to get no immediate share of his father's legacy, which consisted of seventy-one shares of business stock worth about two thousand dollars.

The next five years were troubled ones, punctuated by financial worries, family deaths, and illness. Deciding on a career in law, Lippard worked as a legal assistant for William Badger and later Ovid F. Johnson, who was the Attorney-General of Pennsylvania from 1839 to 1845. These jobs aroused Lippard's reformist instinct by exposing him to "social life, hidden sins, and iniquities covered with the cloak of authority."[5] During this period Lippard lived briefly with his Aunt Mary, with whom he must have quarreled, for soon he was living like a poor bohemian, drifting through the Philadelphia streets or out to the Wissahickon. Lippard's authorized biographer, John Bell Bouton, gave an obviously romanticized account of his life at this time, claiming that he established squatter's sovereignty in an old abandoned mansion near Franklin Square, a mammoth structure with labyrinthine halls and nearly a hundred rooms. A more realistic appraisal is that he stayed in the studios of artist friends and occasionally in vacant buildings.

As disillusioned with the law as he had been with the ministry, the eighteen-year-old Lippard in 1840 began writing his first long romance, *The Ladye Annabel,* which he would not complete until 1843. In the fall of 1841 Lippard was living in a garret with an artist when he was introduced to John S. DuSolle, the editor of a lively Philadelphia penny newspaper called the *Spirit of the Times.*[6] DuSolle put Lippard to work rewriting clipped articles from other papers, and then as a city news reporter. Between January and early April 1842 Lippard contributed to DuSolle's paper three daily columns, numerous local news stories, and two Oriental allegories.

In his pieces for the *Spirit of the Times* Lippard tested several literary voices and themes that later he would develop more extensively in his novels. In the "Our Talisman" series he created a wryly commonsensical character, Flib, who had the power of becoming invisible and witnessing the secretly corrupt activities of bank presidents, theater managers, and other "respectable" types. In his semifictional "City Police" columns he assumed the persona of "Billy Brier" to report the arrest and trial of a wide variety of figures—hellfire preachers, drunken politicians, prostitutes, and even literary characters such as Hamlet and the Wandering Jew. Elsewhere in DuSolle's paper Lippard editorialized against the recent acquittal of Nicholas Biddle, the United States Bank president who had been brought to trial on conspiracy charges, and against the misappropriation of the legacy of the philanthropist Stephen Girard, who at his death in 1831 had left $2 million for a college for orphans that was still not built in 1842 and would not be completed until 1848. In addition, Lippard launched witty attacks on several members of the American literary establishment. His most popular columns, "The Sanguine Poetaster" and "The Bread Crust Papers," satirized two popular poets, Henry B. Hirst and Thomas Dunn English, as lisping fops and sophomoric versifiers. In his reports of Charles Dickens's American tour, which he wrote with DuSolle, Lippard mocked the literati of New York and Philadelphia who were honoring

"Boz" with grand feasts and award ceremonies. The "insipid adulation" by these "Boz-Bedlamites" repelled the intensely patriotic Lippard, who correctly predicted that Dickens would write an unflattering portrait of Americans upon his return to England.[7]

In April 1842 Lippard quit the *Spirit of the Times*, deciding to embark wholeheartedly upon a career as a fiction-writer. His first story, "Philippe de Agramont," appeared on July 9, 1842, in the *Saturday Evening Post*. This tale was a medieval Gothic thriller about the peasant revolt led by Wat Tyler in 1381 against King Richard II, who had oppressively taxed the poor. Lippard's next work, a novel about the American Revolution called *Herbert Tracy, or The Legend of the Black Rangers*, ran serially in the *Post* between October 22 and November 26, 1842, not to appear in book form until 1844. The first of Lippard's many historical "legends" that combined fact and fancy, *Herbert Tracy* used the Wissahickon countryside and Revolutionary battles as backdrops to a competition between a Tory and a poor patriot for the love of an American woman. *Herbert Tracy* met "with popular favor as signal as it was unexpected" and was extensively reprinted in newspapers throughout the nation.[8]

In January 1843 Lippard went to work for his friends Isaac and Adam Diller as an anonymous editor and writer for the *Citizen Soldier: A Weekly Newspaper Devoted to the Interests of the Volunteers and Militia of the United States*. By May Lippard had become the paper's main writer and by July its chief editor. His piquant literary criticism and highly charged narratives were an immediate success with the public, causing a dramatic rise in the paper's circulation. Especially popular were his "Spermaceti Papers" and "Walnut Coffin Papers," in which he caricatured various members of Philadelphia's leading periodical publishing firm, George R. Graham and Company. Among those portrayed were "Spermaceti Sam" (Samuel P. Patterson, copublisher of the *Saturday Evening Post*), "Professor Peter Sun" (Charles J. Peterson, a prolific and careless writer of magazine fiction), "The Reverend Rumpus Grizzle" (Rufus Wilmot Griswold, the famous anthologist and editor), and "The Grey Ham" himself. Using vernacular satire in a way that would be perfected by Mark Twain, Lippard described these men as self-important country bumpkins who palmed off sentimental poetry and fiction as "American Literature." While exhibiting ingenuity in his attack on the Graham group, Lippard showed discrimination in praising Charles Brockden Brown, James Fenimore Cooper, and Washington Irving. Lippard's highest praise went to Edgar Allan Poe, whom he had probably known since the spring of 1842. "Delighting in the wild and visionary," he said of Poe, "his mind penetrates the utmost recesses of the human soul, creating vast and magnificent dreams, eloquent fancies and terrible mysteries." Lippard commended Poe's criticism as well as his verse and fiction, and acutely saw worth in the neglected *Arthur Gordon Pym,* which "disclose[s] perceptive and descriptive powers that rival DeFoe, combined with an analytical depth of reasoning in no manner inferior to Godwin or Charles Brockden Brown."[9]

An entertaining and often perceptive literary critic, the twenty-one-year-old Lippard was also proving himself a remarkably prolific, crowd-pleasing fictionist and essayist. In the brief year that he was the principal writer for the *Citizen Soldier,* he contributed to the paper several Revolutionary legends, some timely essays on recent political events, a religious story, and two Gothic narratives, which included the story "Adrian the Neophyte" and the novel *The Ladye Annabel; or, The Doom of the Poisoner.* His most popular pieces were "The Men of the Revolution," "The Battle-Day of Germantown," and "The Battle-Day of Brandywine," in which he clothed historical fact with semifanciful oral traditions about supernatural prophecies and battlefield heroism. Lippard's "Jesus the Democrat" gave an innovatively political, humanistic coloring to the Christ story, while "Adrian the Neophyte" cynically traced the collapse of a medieval monk's faith in the face of sexual passion. Lippard's longest *Citizen Soldier* piece, *The Ladye Annabel,* the last purely Gothic narrative he ever wrote, was a witches' brew of medieval torture, live burials, violent political revolution, alchemy, grisly dreams of hell, and necrophilia.

By early 1844 Lippard's fiction had gained wide popularity but little critical attention or praise. The many enthusiastic reviews of Lippard's work appearing in the *Citizen Soldier* were written by Lippard himself, or by his friends and employers, the Dillers. The critics who did take notice of Lippard generally branded him as a vigorous but chaotic and indecent writer.

Hoping to buttress his respectability, he sent a copy of *The Ladye Annabel* to his friend Poe for evaluation. On February 18, 1844, Poe sent a letter of reply:

My dear Lippard—

It will give me pleasure to attend to what you suggest. In a day or two you shall hear from me further.

Touching the "Ladye Annabel," I regret that, until lately, I could find no opportunity of giving it a thorough perusal. The opinion I expressed to you, personally, was based, as I told you, upon a very cursory examination. It has been confirmed, however, by a subsequent reading at leisure. You seem to have been in too desperate a hurry to give due attention to details; and thus your style, although generally nervous, is at times somewhat exuberant—but the work, as a whole, will be admitted, by all but your personal enemies, to be richly inventive and imaginative—indicative of *genius* in its author.

And as for these personal enemies, I cannot see that you need put yourself to any especial trouble about THEM. Let a fool alone—especially if he be both a scoundrel and a fool—and he will kill himself far sooner than you can kill him by any active exertion. Besides—as to the real philosophy of the thing—you should regard the small animosities—the animosities of small men—of the literary animiculae (who have their uses, beyond doubt)—as so many tokens of your ascent—or, rather, as so many stepping stones to your ambition. I have never yet been able to make up my mind whether I regard as the higher compliment, the approbation of a man of honor and talent, or the abuse of an ass or a blackguard. Both are excellent in their way—for a man who looks steadily up.

If my opinion of "The Ladye Annabel" can be of *any* service to you whatever, you have my full permission to publish this letter, or any portion of it you may deem proper.

With respect and friendship,
Yours,
Edgar A. Poe

Pleased with the letter, Lippard published it in March 1844 as an epilogue to his novel *Herbert Tracy,* noting in "A Word to the Reader" that Poe was "universally confessed one of the most gifted men in the land."[10]

Five Controversial Years (1844–1849)

From the time he quit the *Citizen Soldier* in the spring of 1844 until late 1849, when he devoted himself primarily to the Brotherhood of the Union, Lippard was periodically embroiled in heated literary and political controversies. The 1830s and 1840s were turbulent decades for Philadelphia—a time of church burnings, religious and racial riots, severe economic depression, labor strikes, Millerite prophecies of impending doom, and fierce gang warfare. Lippard stepped into this stormy urban arena like a literary warrior, brandishing his sword of fiction against upperclass hypocrites and sectarian bigots while defending the poor in the name of "the Carpenter of Nazareth," George Washington, and, later, the French socialists. His fiction during this period was full of lively commentary on nearly every current reform or philosophical fad: abolition, women's rights, magnetism, mesmerism, astrology, Millerism, capital punishment, spirit knocking, Catholicism and anti-Catholicism, socialism, and the political revolutions in Europe. While bringing to American literature a fresh topicality and political fervor, Lippard continued to fabricate seminal myths about the early-Christian and American past. Although his fiction, which was now earning him some $3,000 to $4,000 annually, was consumed ravenously by the public and praised increasingly by critics, it was also widely pilloried, pirated, and plagiarized, impelling him to lash out against those literary "insects" and "reptiles" that he thought were ignoring his moral mission and exploiting his popularity.

This five-year period began staidly enough for Lippard, who spent much of the summer of 1844 laying plans for a semimonthly periodical, *Lippard's Magazine of Historical Romance,* devoted "to the cause of a distinct and individual National Literature."[11] In August Lippard wrote to Robert Morris, a well-known Philadelphia poet and essayist, and to James Fenimore Cooper, requesting their endorsement of his new project. With characteristic ambition Lippard explained that every second number of the forty-six-page magazine would contain a new novel "illustrative of some remarkable American Battle-field or some appropriate event of olden time."[12] Apparently Morris and Cooper were uninterested, for the proposed magazine never appeared, and not until 1849 would Lippard's dream of managing his own periodical reach fruition.

If the summer of 1844 was a quiet season of futile plans, fall and winter were a hectic time of notoriety and public furor created by Lippard's new and most famous novel, *The Quaker City; or, The Monks of Monk Hall. A Romance of Philadelphia Life, Mystery and Crime.* For all its racy scandal sheets, sensational penny papers, and imported French novels, Philadelphia had never seen the likes of *The Quaker City.* Lippard's main plot was familiar to many, for it was based on a famous trial of 1843 in which a Philadelphian named Singleton Mercer was acquitted after killing Mahlon Heberton, who had enticed Mercer's sister into a house of assignation and allegedly raped her at gunpoint. Onto this real-life scandal Lippard grafted various literary elements—the pornographic titillation of nativist fiction which ascribed horrific practices to foreign emigrants, the supernaturalism and violent grotesquerie of the Gothic novel, the democratic antielitism of the penny press and French fiction, colorful Dickensian caricature—to produce a serial novel with instant appeal for the mass audience. The ten paper-covered installments of the novel appearing between the fall of 1844 and the spring of 1845 sold at a record-breaking pace. When the first two-thirds of the novel were bound together after six months, 48,000 copies were bought. When in May 1845 the whole expanded version appeared, with a dedication to Charles Brockden Brown and engravings by DeWitt C. Hitchcock and F. O. C. Darley, the publishers reported that more than 60,000 copies had been sold within a year.

According to John Bell Bouton, *The Quaker City* divided Philadelphia into two camps, with poor laborers taking Lippard's side.[13] The city was buzzing with guesses about which local celebrities Lippard was trying to expose in his various subplots, and Lippard talked of threats made on his life. In November 1844, when only a few of the ten serial segments had appeared, a local paper was running ads for "The Monk Hall Cigars . . . Fresh from Monk Hall."[14]

Also in November Lippard signed a contract with Francis C. Wemyss, the manager of the Chesnut Street Theater, to furnish a dramatized version of *The Quaker City*. Lippard wrote a play, which went into rehearsal and was scheduled for performance on November 11. When the playbills were put up, however, Singleton Mercer, displeased by Lippard's notably qualified portrayal of him, defaced a bill that was posted outside the theater while a jeering crowd gathered to watch. Mercer then applied for two hundred tickets "for the purpose of a grand row" and threats were heard that the theater would be sacked or burned.[15] Alarmed by this growing agitation, Wemyss decided to postpone the performance and then, after consulting the mayor of Philadelphia and the state deputy attorney-general, to cancel it. On November 11 an unruly crowd, angry about the cancellation, gathered outside the theater, with the whole city police force trying to keep order. Lippard, who later said he was armed with a sword-cane and pistols to repel assaults, reportedly helped to pacify the crowd by giving a speech.[16] When a substitute play was proposed, the mob finally dispersed. Wemyss was deeply disturbed by the whole affair. Not only was his reputation sullied, but he thought the play was "really a good one [that] would have secured a run."[17] After watching a pirated play based on *The Quaker City* in New York in January 1845, however, Wemyss declared that he "could not recognize a line" in this "mass of filth and obscenity" (398).

The Chesnut Street Theater affair was wonderful publicity and encouraged the first publisher of *The Quaker City,* George B. Zieber, to sign a new contract giving Lippard a salary of five dollars a week for three months, plus half of the publisher's profits from a greatly expanded version of the novel which Lippard completed early in 1845.

Critical response to Lippard's novel was mixed. The local press generally praised it. The *Philadelphia Home Journal* called it "the

first American work which, written with the intention of illustrating the secrets of life in our large cities, has met with the
decided approval of the public."[18] The *Saturday Courier* lauded
Lippard's insights into the human soul. In Boston Theodore Parker found "scenes of great power and unexceptionable excellence"
in *The Quaker City*.[19] Lippard received ambiguous plaudits from
as far away as England, where in London the *New Monthly Magazine* called his novel "one of the most remarkable that has
emanated from the new world."[20]

These voices, however, were drowned out by the protest against
what was called the novel's obscenity and libelous intent. Lippard's former employer, John S. DuSolle, charged Lippard with
writing "a disgusting mass of filth" and with trying to blackmail
prominent Philadelphians.[21] In London the *Athenaeum* declared
that Lippard dealt with "atrocities too horrid for belief."[22] In
response to charges that he had written "the most immoral work
of the age," Lippard insisted that he was a moral crusader who
depicted sex and violence only to expose them.[23]

The critical debate over Lippard's "immorality" raged for years.
Meanwhile, *The Quaker City* continued to sell well, passing
through twenty-seven "editions" by 1849 and enjoying a lively
sale abroad. In 1846 the popular German novelist Friedrich Gerstäcker claimed authorship of *Die Quackerstadt und ihre Geheimnisse*,
a translation of Lippard's novel that passed through three editions
in as many months. Two years later another pirated version of
The Quaker City was printed in London under the title of *Dora
Livingstone, the Adulteress; or, The Quaker City*.

In America the success of Lippard's work and of Eugene Sue's
The Mysteries of Paris (1842–1843) gave impetus to a whole school
of popular fiction about the "mysteries and miseries" of American
cities. Some fifty American novels of city life, most of which
exaggerated Lippard's sensationalism while leaving out his reformist purpose and psychological themes, appeared between
1844 and 1860; Ned Buntline, Henri Foster, and George Thompson established themselves as the most prolific and opportunistic
authors in the field. The corrupt aristocracy and squalid poverty
of New York, Boston, and Philadelphia were the most popular

topics, though the city novelists investigated a remarkable array of other American cities, including Rochester, Lowell, Nashua, St. Louis, New Orleans, and San Francisco. One of these novels, A. J. H. Duganne's *Mysteries of the Three Cities* (1845), included a plot about "George Davenant" (Lippard), a poor long-haired Philadelphian who first worked for "Stephen Soleil's *Eau de Temps*" (DuSolle's *Spirit of the Times*) and then went on to "rail at the world" in his exposé of Philadelphia.[24] Henri Foster's *Ellen Grafton. The Den of Crime* (1850) was one of three obvious imitations of *The Quaker City,* and other city novels either directly quoted Lippard's work or blatantly lifted devices from it.

After the initial furor over *The Quaker City* had died down, Lippard resumed writing legends of the American Revolution. On December 8, 1845, he gave the first of many patriotic lectures before the William Wirt Institute, a local historical association, and in 1846 and 1847 he divided his time between writing fiction and lecturing throughout Pennsylvania and as far away as Virginia, Maryland, and Georgia. An impassioned and riveting speaker, Lippard was in constant demand. Within fifteen months he gave some fifty lectures, and two Pennsylvania colleges, Penna College of Gettysburg and Jefferson College of Cannonsburg, elected him to their honorary philosophical societies.

Most of Lippard's lectures were versions of legends that he was writing for Philadelphia's most popular weekly, the *Saturday Courier.* Lippard had been periodically contributing legends to the *Courier* since 1845, and between his commencement of a new series of sixty-two "Legends of the Revolution" in July 1846 and the completion of the series on December 23, 1848, the *Courier's* weekly circulation leapt from 30,000 to 70,000. According to the paper's editor, Andrew M'Makin, Lippard's Revolutionary stories were "more generally copied by the entire press of the country than any other series that ever appeared in the Courier."[25] This "perfectly inimitable and wonderfully popular series," M'Makin boasted, had led several critics to characterize Lippard as "a writer of great originality and extraordinary nerve" comparable "to some of the most powerful writers of Europe."[26] In addition to the legends, Lippard contributed to the *Courier* a new novel called *Blanche of Brandywine,* which combined a bloody account of the Revolutionary battle of Brandywine with a story of romantic intrigue involving two American women pursued by lecherous British soldiers and defended by heroic Americans.

At the same time that Lippard's popularity was increasing, his graphic fiction continued to draw fire from some critics. On August 5, 1846, the *Saturday Evening Post,* which had published Lippard's first story in 1842, lambasted him as a "pernicious" writer of "the French school," initiating a long journalistic debate between the *Post* and the *Courier* over the worth of his fiction. Lippard responded by writing a lengthy article for the *Courier,* "George Lippard: His Opponents and the Public," in which he stressed his moral intentions and popular support. The *Post* answered with an editorial on "Immoral Books," dubbing Lippard the chief of *"the raw head and bloody bones school"* of literature. Quoting a racy passage from *The Quaker City,* this piece charged Lippard with arousing "the wanton devil that lies sleeping in every human heart" and gilding "robust licentiousness" with "namby-pamby sentimentalities about the beauty of virtue, and heaven and hell."[27] It also questioned the validity of Lippard's Revolutionary legends, especially his story of the dying Thomas Paine's conversion to Christianity.

Lippard's quarrel with the *Post* lasted into the early months of 1847. Meanwhile, in the fall of 1846 Lippard had formed his own publishing firm to issue a sequel to *The Quaker City* called *The Nazarene,* in which he attacked Calvinist nativists and exploitative businessmen while defending Philadelphia's poor seamstresses and the victimized Indians on the western frontier. After just five of the projected twenty-four serial installments of *The Nazarene* had appeared, to the dismay of his readers Lippard quit writing the novel, probably because he was so busy lecturing and writing legends for the *Courier.* George Lippard and Company went bankrupt because of its owner's failure to complete the novel, though Zieber's subsequent edition of the unfinished book was quite popular.

1847 and 1848 were heady years for Lippard. He was at the zenith of his popularity as an author and lecturer, and his hopes for the success of the European political revolutions were exceeded only by his adoration of his "child-wife," Rose. Lippard had courted the shy and affectionate Rose Newman for several years, and had documented his claim to her on New Year's Day in 1844, when he gave her a pocket Bible with a signed, poetic inscription— ". . . maiden, I am thine, and maiden thou art mine." On May 15, 1847, the two were married by moonlight on a high rock overlooking the Wissahickon, with Lippard's friend the Universalist clergyman Charles Chauncey Burr conducting a simple ceremony witnessed only by Lippard's sister Harriet.

1847 also saw the appearance of three more Lippard volumes: *Washington and His Generals,* a collection of Revolutionary legends, most of which had previously been published separately or had been used as lectures; *The Rose of Wissahikon,* a relatively benign novelette about the Revolution with a dedication to Lippard's wife; and *Legends of Mexico,* a celebration of Zachary Taylor's recent campaigns below the Rio Grande. Early in the year Lippard wrote a political drama, *The Sons of Temperance,* which had a long run at Peale's Museum. In the spring Mrs. H. M. Ward's dramatic adaptation of *Blanche of Brandywine,* advertised as "the first domestic drama on the Revolution ever played in this country," played before packed houses in local theaters.[28] Also in the spring Lippard for the first time engaged actively in politics. After campaigning as an Independent Democrat for the office of District Commissioner of Philadelphia, he lost to a regular Democrat in a close election.

Despite his literary productivity and domestic bliss during 1847, Lippard continued to generate controversy. When Joel Tyler Headley's *Washington and His Generals* appeared at about the same time as Lippard's work of the same name, Lippard, in a series of articles for the *Saturday Courier* beginning May 15, accused Headley of plagiarism. Lippard began by declaring that he had been "the victim of such petty larcenies for years," and that "the very men who have clamored loudest about my immorality, have manifested their sincerity by appropriating whole pages from my books" (*Courier,* May 15, 1847). He carefully documented his claim against Headley and against three other "pilferers" as well. After waiting for a reply from Headley, he repeated the charge on July 12 and again on November 27. Incensed by Headley's silence, he turned on another plagiarist, Friedrich Gerstäcker, whose pirated translation of *The Quaker City* had just come to his attention. Of Gerstäcker Lippard said: "Here is a Dutch Headley, with a vengeance, who takes not only part of my book, but takes it all, and puts his [name] on the cover" (*Courier,* November 27, 1847).

This combined spirit of zestful activity and heated controversy carried over into 1848. Charles Chauncey Burr, who in September 1847 had penned a long paean to Lippard's "Shakespearian" genius, asked Lippard to contribute to his lively new reformist quarterly, the *Nineteenth Century.* In 1848 and 1849 six pieces by Lippard appeared in Burr's periodical, including a warm tribute to Charles Brockden Brown, with whom Lippard felt a deep kinship. Two more books by Lippard were published in 1848— *'Bel of Prairie Eden,* an adventure novel about the West, and *Paul Ardenheim,* a long, semiautobiographical novel in which a Lippard-like hero was placed in a fantastic Revolutionary War setting with alchemists, pietistic monks, and passionate women.

Although Lippard was now receiving critical applause in small-town newspapers in many parts of the nation, the major eastern journals were still ignoring him while middlebrow sheets were poking fun at him. The *John-Donkey,* a New York humor weekly, described Lippard's *"Romantic High-Pressure Highfaluting Style"* as "a compound of Eugene Sue, Mrs. Radcliffe, 'La Belle Assemblee,' and the Lunatic Asylum." The *John-Donkey* review included a set of mock rules for the person who wished to write like Lippard: attend a melodrama at the Chatham Street Theater, "where you'll learn gory, horrible, shrieking, bloody plots"; go home and tousle your hair, rip open your shirt, and upset all the furniture; get a huge tablet of "imperial paper," an iron pen, and "at least a gallon of black ink"; and then write feverishly about medieval torture, heaving bosoms, and horses hurtling over cliffs.[29] *Holden's Dollar Magazine,* also of New York, said Lippard was using literary "brimstone, saltpetre, and kreosote" to "tickle the palate of our copper-throated public," producing fiction that was "a most delectable hash of horror, superstition and ribaldry, equalled in point of variety and cookery, by nothing but the witch-kettle of Macbeth."[30]

If Lippard was aware of such jibes, he was too busy to respond to them, for he was becoming embroiled in national politics. The European revolutions of February 1848 spurred him to look into the works of such French socialists as Charles Fourier, Louis Blanc, and Ledru Rollin. When the National Reform Congress, an annual gathering of labor activists, met in Philadelphia in June, Lippard gave a valedictory address defending land reform, homestead exemption, and the rights of labor. On July 5 he wrote to the Whig presidential candidate Zachary Taylor, whom he regarded as the poor man's hero, asking for assurance that Taylor was "the candidate, not of a party" but "of the whole people."[31] After Taylor had sent him a one-line reply giving this assurance, Lippard spent much of the fall stumping Pennsylvania for Taylor, whose victory in the state helped him win the national election in November. By March 1849, however, after an interview with the new president in Washington, Lippard felt deeply betrayed, for Taylor was surrounding himself with Whig politicians and aspersing the European revolutionaries.

If Lippard was disappointed with Taylor, he was even more saddened by the deaths in December 1848 of his beloved sister Harriet and Harry Diller, his friend from the *Citizen Soldier* days. But these tragedies did not paralyze Lippard, who at last realized his long-standing dream of founding his own periodical. After securing the support of a local publisher of popular literature, Joseph Severns, Lippard came out with the first issue of the *Quaker City* weekly on December 30, 1848, and ran this oversized family paper—its printed pages were two feet deep and nearly three feet wide—almost singlehandedly until its last issue appeared on June 8, 1850. Long resentful of profit-making publishers and salaried editors who stood between him and the public, Lippard saw in his new weekly an opportunity for reaping the full financial fruits of his writing while advancing "social reform through the medium of popular literature."[32]

The *Quaker City* weekly was nearly as successful as his novel of the same name, for by May 1849 he could claim a circulation of 10,000, a figure that had nearly doubled by the end of the summer. Every week, in addition to fiction and reformist essays, he printed excerpts from complimentary reviews of his work, such as Park Benjamin's judgment that Lippard was "the Eugene Sue of America, possessing graphic powers which even excel those of the great French novelist," or the comment in *Godey's Lady's Book* that "This author has struck out on an entirely new path, and stands isolated on a point inaccessible to the mass of writers of the present day. He is unquestionably the most popular writer of the day, and his books are sold, edition after edition, thousand after thousand, while those of others accumulate, like useless lumber, on the shelves of the publishers."[33]

1849 was Lippard's most prolific year as a writer. In the *Quaker City* weekly appeared five new serial novels by Lippard: *The Memoirs of a Preacher* and its sequel *The Man with the Mask,* which exposed the immorality of some popular preachers while commenting topically on women's rights, magnetism, slavery, and Millerism; *The Entranced, or the Wanderer of Eighteen Centuries,* a socialist fictionalization of history from early-Christian times to 1848, the "sacred" year of the European revolutions; *The Empire City,* which pictured debauchery and corruption among New York's moneyed elite; and *The Killers,* a portrayal of gang warfare in Philadelphia based on the election-night riots of October 9, 1849. Lippard also wrote for his weekly a new series of Revolutionary legends that later were collected as *Washington and His Men* (1850), as well as "Legends of Every Day," humanitarian portraits of poor families exploited by the rich. In miscellaneous essays Lippard endorsed homestead exemption, election reform, and militant labor combination. In "The Quaker City Police Court" Lippard portrayed a "Justice Poe" passing judgment on sentimental writers and corrupt celebrities.

Lippard's continued admiration for Poe was apparently reciprocated by Poe's trust in him, for on July 12, 1849, the impoverished Poe, having wandered for two weeks through Philadelphia seeking monetary assistance from old literary associates, came to

Lippard's *Quaker City* office begging for help. Lippard later re-called that Poe, hungry and desperate, told him, "You are my last hope. If you fail me, I can do nothing but die."[34] The next day Lippard went around Philadelphia collecting some eleven dollars from various authors and publishers. This money helped save Poe from starvation, and a train ticket bought by Charles Chauncey Burr enabled the poet to reach Baltimore, where he took a boat to Richmond, arriving there on July 14 with two dollars to spare. In a letter of July 19 to his mother Poe wrote, "To L[ippard] and to C[hauncey] B[urr] . . . I am indebted for more than life."[35] When Lippard got the news of Poe's death on October 7, he wrote a moving eulogy of this wronged "man of genius" and later became one of the first writers of the day to attack the misrepresentation of Poe in Rufus Griswold's preface to the collected edition of Poe's works.[36]

Brotherhood, Tragedy, and Death

His busiest year as a writer, 1849 was also the time when Lippard fulfilled another dream by founding an organization de-voted to the cause of labor. The Brotherhood of the Union was Lippard's ultimate attempt at bringing together various ideas and reforms that had increasingly preoccupied him since the early 1840s: the ritualism of ancient orders such as the Druids, the Rosicrucians, and the Illuminati; the intense patriotism, without the nativism, of the Masons and the Odd Fellows; the nonsectarian religious tolerance best exemplified by his Universalist friend Burr; and principles of reform, deriving in part from Utopian Socialism, that called for radical revision of the capitalist system. In Lippard's words, the Brotherhood was designed to "espouse the cause of the Masses, and battle against the tyrants of the Social System,—against corrupt Bankers, against Land Monop-olists and against all Monied Oppressors." If peaceful reform fails, "then we advise Labor to go to War, in any and all forms—War with the Rifle, Sword and Knife" (*QCW,* October 29, 1849).

After the first notice of Lippard's newly formed Brotherhood appeared in the *Quaker City* weekly on July 21, 1849, the order grew with astonishing speed. By mid-September requests for

charters were flooding in from all over Pennsylvania and surrounding states, and from several states in the South and West,
including Tennessee, Arkansas, Illinois, Michigan, and Ohio.
Fearing "the corrupting influence of Large Cities," Lippard at
first granted charters only to rural towns, though this proscription
relaxed as the Brotherhood grew (*QCW,* December 12, 1849).
By the time of the order's First Annual Convocation in October
1850, 142 circles had been formed in nineteen states. The central
governing unit consisted of a Supreme Circle of fifty-six members
(duplicating the number of signers of the Declaration of Independence) and an inner circle of thirteen (the number of original
American states), while Grand Circles operated on the state or
district levels. The chief officers of the Brotherhood were des-
ignated Washington, Jefferson, Franklin, Wayne, Fulton, and
Girard, with "Supreme" appearing before each title. Ritual par-
aphernalia included "a large Magic Lantern," an "Indian cos-
tume," "Collars of Merino, Robes of Cambric," urns, and
torches.[37]

Historians have long overlooked Lippard's importance in the
American labor movement. In the early 1850s the Brotherhood
of the Union became a tightly structured national organization
that synthesized various reforms: land reform, Fourierism, co-
operation, election reform, and subversive anticapitalism derived
mainly from French secret societies. George Henry Evans, the
leading land reformer of the day, predicted that Lippard's "noble
and glorious" order would become "one of the most powerful
instrumentalities in restoring the land to the people" (quoted in
QCW, February 2, 1850). Several of Evans's followers, including
the prominent agrarians John Commerford and Gilbert Vale, Jr.,
became members of the Brotherhood. America's foremost advo-
cate of Fourierism, Albert Brisbane, lectured to a New York
circle of the Brotherhood in 1850. In addition to endorsing land
reform and certain aspects of Fourierism, Lippard was a moving
force in the ascendant cooperative movement. In March 1850 he
founded a cooperative store for Philadelphia seamstresses that set
the pattern for an important New York tailors' cooperative formed
that summer. He was also closely associated with the Daughters

and Sons of Toil, an extremely radical group of Philadelphia reformers who ran a carpet cooperative and who supported women's suffrage, rights for blacks and Native Americans, and a wholesale revision of the capitalist system that verged on syndicalism. At the same time, Lippard worked earnestly for the *Arbeiterbund,* the German workingmen's league run by the utopian communist Wilhelm Weitling.

Perhaps most significantly, Lippard's Brotherhood was a precursor of the Noble and Holy Order of the Knights of Labor, which would be founded in Philadelphia in 1867 by Uriah S. Stephens and would by 1886 become the most powerful labor organization in the country. Lippard's vision of a secret, universal brotherhood embracing workers of all trades and creeds in mystical oneness under a fatherly God anticipated the outlook of Stephens, who, having lived in Philadelphia when Lippard was at his height, was "strongly influenced" by the younger labor leader.[38]

Lippard devoted the last years of his life (1850–1854) primarily to reform activity and only sporadically to writing fiction. In October 1850 the Brotherhood elected him Supreme Washington, a post he held for life.

At first this was an exuberant period for Lippard, but family deaths, money problems, and trouble within the Brotherhood increasingly darkened the picture. His gloom over the death in October 1849 of his young daughter Mima was in part dispelled by the birth of a son, Paul, in May 1850, but within ten months the boy was gone, too. The hardest blow came when his wife, Rose, died of tuberculosis in the spring of 1851, at the age of twenty-six. Since the day of Rose's death, Lippard later wrote, "I have not known a moment's peace, or been at home in any place. A more miserable man, or one so stripped and bereaved, you never saw."[39] Shortly after Rose died Lippard was said to have attempted suicide by leaping into Niagara Falls, and was saved by a friend who pulled him back just in time.

Lippard sought refuge from his grief in frenzied work for the Brotherhood. He wrote a two-hundred-page ritual book for the order entitled *The B. G. C.,* which he called "the most arduous labor of my life." Since no complete copy of *The B. G. C.* has survived, there is no way of testing Lippard's claim that it was "the fullest and most copious ritual of any secret society in the world."[40] In July 1851 Lippard published *The White Banner,* a collection of his recent writings and Brotherhood news of which only one number was published.

Whatever gratification Lippard got from such writing was diminished by his realization that his authorship was no longer a guarantee of best sellers. To pay Brotherhood debts he had been forced to sell the plates of his five novels of 1849, and he mused that the time and labor expended on *The B. G. C., "if applied in the usual channel of authorship . . . would have benefitted me to the amount of thousands of dollars" ("Brotherhood Notes," 4). His plans for subsequent editions of *The White Banner* were foiled when certain members of the Brotherhood wrongly accused him of writing the magazine for private gain. By 1852 he could talk of "traitors" in the Brotherhood, which he said was plagued with "difficulties within, and opposition from without" ("Brotherhood Notes," 7). Nevertheless, the Brotherhood continued to grow, and in 1852 and 1853 Lippard traveled hundreds of miles lecturing on its behalf throughout Pennsylvania, New York, New England, and as far away as Ohio, Maryland, and Virginia. He lectured mainly on Revolutionary heroes and social reform, but also on the Bible and on spiritualism, which had fascinated him since the famous Fox sisters' "rappings" in 1848.

While Lippard's literary output declined during this period, it did not cease completely. Late in 1852 Charles Chauncey Burr and his brother Heman made Lippard the literary editor of their new daily, the *New York National Democrat.* Lippard held this post for a few months, writing sketches of corrupt New York aristocrats that provided the basis for a volume of short stories called *The Midnight Queen.* In the summer of 1853 Lippard took a break from his lecturing to write a story, "A Turnpike and a Divorce," for *Scott's Weekly,* and later in the year his longest work of the period, *New York: Its Upper Ten and Lower Million* was published in Cincinnati—the furthest West he ever traveled— and "met with a prompt and extensive sale."[41] In *New York,* a novel he had been working on for three years, he resurrected several characters from an earlier work, *The Empire City,* to launch attacks on family concentrations of wealth, on slavery, and on an alleged attempt by Roman Catholics to infiltrate American schools and government.

Predictably, Lippard did not cease to stir up controversy. In the spring of 1852, at a dinner following his lecture at an Odd Fellows' lodge in Virginia, Lippard, overhearing angry whispers about his antislavery views, toasted his hosts pugnaciously: "Here's to the revolving pistol. The best antidote to a Northern scoundrel who meddles with the opinion of a Southern Gentleman upon slavery while traveling in the North; and an equally good course of treatment for a Southern blackguard who interferes with the sentiments of a Northerner while a guest of the South."[42] Also, he was still fighting with critics and plagiarists. He sent a sharp retort to one Philadelphia magazine for its negative review of *The Midnight Queen,* and he accused another of printing "A Turnpike and a Divorce" under a different title without his permission. In 1853 Lippard wrote a letter of protest to a Philadelphia committee that was proposing to erect a monument to Benjamin Franklin. Always for the underdog, he argued that Franklin was well commemorated and that a monument should be dedicated instead to a lesser-known American hero, such as the neglected steamboat inventor John Fitch. Partly because of his involvement, the Franklin monument was never built.

Despite continued activity, Lippard in 1853 was sinking into a depressed and morbid state. On June 25 he predicted in a letter to a friend that he would die within a year of consumption, a prediction that proved accurate. He spent the summer, which he said was to be his last, lecturing in Ohio and taking a steamboat tour of the Great Lakes. After returning to Philadelphia to oversee the Fourth Annual Convocation of the Brotherhood in October, he developed a strange phobia against omnibuses and an even stranger belief that he was dying not of consumption but of a liver ailment. In a letter to Heman Burr he predicted that he would be dead by March 1854, an even more accurate prediction than his previous one. On December 5 a friend suggested that a water cure might relieve his "declining health and extreme depression of spirits," but by this time he was confined to his house, beyond hope of cure.[43] Early in 1854 two lady spiritualists came to Lippard's home offering him a potion they said had been sent by celestial spirits to cure him. He refused the potion, pointing to a statuette of Christ on his bedroom shelf and declaring, "That's the spirit I believe in."[44]

Though prostrated with illness, in January 1854 Lippard was busy writing a long serial story for the *Philadelphia Sunday Mercury* called "Eleanor; or, Slave Catching in the Quaker City," a protest against the Fugitive Slave Law of 1850. When his doctor warned him that he was too ill to write, he sketched some twenty stories in pictures, including one about his departed wife, Rose. He was still out of bed scribbling on February 8, but early the next morning he weakened and died. According to his sister Sarah, his last words were, "Lord Jesus, receive my spirit."[45]

Lippard's funeral on February 13 was a grand affair led by members of his Brotherhood and by the Odd Fellows and Free-Masons. Hundreds of German Americans, to whom Lippard had become a kind of folk hero, thronged with Brotherhood members and other friends to witness the procession to Odd Fellows Cemetery, where Lippard was laid to rest. Several local papers eulogized him. The *Public Ledger* called him "the author of a number of novels, which have been read probably as extensively as those of any writer in this country."[46] The *Sunday Mercury* judged that "his memory will live, his genius will live, and future ages will recognize his works while here, as a bright and good inheritance."[47]

From a literary standpoint the *Sunday Mercury*'s prophecy proved wrong, for before long Lippard's fiction sank into obscurity, and reprintings of selected Lippard novels in 1860, 1864, and 1876 failed to restore the best-selling writer of the 1840s to popularity. Several of Lippard's Revolutionary legends became a part of American folklore, but the creator of the legends was virtually forgotten, and by the twentieth century his novels were gathering dust in scattered scholarly libraries.

However, Lippard's memory did live among members of the Brotherhood of the Union (later renamed the Brotherhood of

America). The turmoil of the Civil War caused a momentary shrinkage of the Brotherhood, but after the war the order expanded rapidly. In 1867 the Rose Lippard Home Communion, a sister organization endorsing women's rights, was formed, with "Rose Lippard" being placed above "Martha Washington" and "Lady Jefferson" in the hierarchy of officer titles. In 1885 a large marble monument was erected in George Lippard's honor in Odd Fellows' Cemetery, and the next year the Brotherhood could boast of one hundred circles in forty states.

As the Brotherhood grew, it lost its original revolutionary fervor, becoming a multimillion-dollar insurance company paying health care and death benefits to its members. In 1900 the Brotherhood, now consisting of 21,278 members divided among 233 circles and homes, reported that more than $3 million in benefits had been awarded since 1875. If the order no longer believed with Lippard that labor should go to war "with the Rifle, Sword and Knife," it nevertheless revered the memory of its founder. At the annual convocation in 1900, four days of festivities were highlighted by a reverential procession to Lippard's grave, where hymns were sung and speeches given in his honor. The Brotherhood reached its numerical peak in 1914, when it claimed more than 30,000 members. The First World War brought a steady decline in membership, which had dropped to 7,837 by 1919 and to 3,140 by 1925. But Lippard was still remembered. On April 15, 1922, the Brotherhood celebrated the centennial of Lippard's birth with another mass pilgrimage to his monument, where a flower was planted on his grave and he was eulogized as a "writer for the poor, defender of the oppressed, enemy of the tyrant, and ever tireless in doing good."[48] At a dinner that night excerpts from several of his novels and essays were read aloud, and his life was discussed.

Only in the 1930s and 1940s, as the Brotherhood continued to dwindle, did the recollection of George Lippard begin to fade. By 1980 the Brotherhood had become a tiny group in Pennsylvania and New Jersey with two hundred members averaging seventy years in age. Just thirty-one members attended a meeting in May 1980, and there was little hope that the order would survive more than a few more years. Lippard's ardent dream of enlisting "all the true men of the Continent" in an organization that would revolutionize America had, like so many of his dreams, fallen into the dustbin of history.[49]

Chapter Two

Beyond Sensationalism: Lippard's Assault on the Rational

Condemned by squeamish critics but loved by the masses, Lippard's sensationalism had roots deep in the literary past and even deeper in the human psyche. Lippard determinedly manipulated the devices of British and French popular fiction in such a way as to generate a vortex of lust, violence, animal savagery, and nightmare.

Sources of Lippard's Sensationalism

In a broad sense Lippard's fiction can be placed in the context of various genres of popular literature that had begun in eighteenth-century England and that spread to France and America in the early decades of the nineteenth century. From the early eighteenth century onward, collections of criminal biography such as *The Newgate Calendar* were immensely popular in England and, after 1800, in America. In the 1780s and 1790s such British writers as Ann Radcliffe, "Monk" Lewis, Horace Walpole, and Clara Reeve popularized the Gothic novel, which usually featured horrific medieval settings, lascivious or bloodthirsty monks, imperiled maidens, and/or supernatural occurrences. Around 1790 the Londoner William Lane founded the Minerva Press, which for several decades disseminated throughout England countless sensational and sentimental tales, many of which found their way to America. The mass production of such fiction was facilitated by the new rotary steam press, invented by John Gamble in 1801 and generally adopted by the publishing industry after 1820. The perfection of the stereotype, making quick reprintings possible, and the development of the lithograph gave further technological impetus to this fiction for the masses.

The period between 1800 and 1840 also saw the rise of the "penny dreadful" in England and the *roman-feuilleton* (the newspaper serial novel) in France. The penny dreadful usually focused on a beautiful, beleaguered heroine who passively depended on a heroic man for rescue from villains. Beneath the moral surface of the penny-dreadful narrative lurked an interest in crime, shock, horror, and sexual aberration for its own sake.[1] The *roman-feuilleton* combined the sensationalism of the penny dreadful with a humanitarian emphasis on the miseries of the poor and the vices of the rich. Appearing in weekly or monthly installments, the *roman-feuilleton* was a virtually structureless, even "styleless" string of fast-paced episodes highlighting terror, suspense, disguise, and sudden plot shifts.[2]

Since nearly all of Lippard's novels appeared serially in paperback or in newspapers, Lippard was following the lead of several established foreign novelists, especially the British William Harrison Ainsworth, Edward Bulwer-Lytton, and G. P. R. James, and the French George Sand and Eugene Sue. By the time Lippard started writing fiction in the early 1840s, Harrison Ainsworth had written eight popular novels about roguish criminals and Gothic villains caught up in whirlwind plots involving hairbreadth escapes, malignant cruelty, and supernaturalism. Bulwer-Lytton and James wrote, in the main, historical fiction that featured a nostalgia for the heroic past and a free embellishment of history with adventurous plots. George Sand, who wrote eighteen novels in the 1830s, pictured a society that through its conventions inhibited truthfulness, spontaneity, and sexual passion in women.[3]

The French novelist who most profoundly influenced Lippard was Eugene Sue, the king of the *roman-feuilleton*. Sue took the penny dreadful out of the drawing room and placed it in the Parisian gutter, teeming with street urchins, prostitutes, thieves, and murderers. For Sue the city was a place of awesome "mysteries," of labyrinthine sewers, dark dens of vice, and backstreet saloons run by ghoulish bartenders—in short, an updated version of that previous literary locus of terror, the Gothic castle. Sue's famous novel, *The Mysteries of Paris* (1842–1843), spawned a host of imitations in England and on the Continent between 1844 and 1860.

In America George Lippard was chiefly responsible for a fifteen-year "city mysteries" craze that had originated in Europe with *The Mysteries of Paris*. The back wrapper of each of the ten original installments of Lippard's *The Quaker City* included the claim: "Commenced before 'Mysteries of Paris' appeared, the Romance, in some respects, bears the same relation to Philadelphia that the 'Mysteries' do to Paris." The first segment of Lippard's novel was greeted with a one-line blurb in the *Public Ledger* announcing in bold letters, "EUGENE SUE ECLIPSED."[4] Lippard often brandished his sobriquet, "The Eugene Sue of America," and devoted several passages in his fiction and essays to defending Sue against his numerous American critics.[5]

Rooted in several kinds of British and Continental fiction, Lippard's sensationalism was also influenced by indigenous phenomena—the penny press, nativist fiction, and the war novel. During the 1830s and 1840s the penny newspapers of America's eastern cities brought about a revolution in American journalism. Papers like the *New York Herald,* the *Boston Daily Times,* and the *Philadelphia Public Ledger* replaced the stuffy partisan six-penny of the past with a new brand of journalism that was democratic, nonpartisan, and above all sensational.[6] Anything lively—a "mysterious disappearance," a "secret tryst," a church burning or murder or bank closure—was fit news to print in the penny papers, which especially enjoyed debunking the rich and respectable. By 1854 one of America's most popular "city mysteries" novelists, George Foster, could write: "The 'penny press,' commencing at the bottom has reached to the very top round of journalism, . . . while the old-fashioned 'respectable six-pennies' are getting farther and farther out of sight and out of mind."[7] Lippard began his career as a writer for a penny paper, DuSolle's *Spirit of the Times,* which had a characteristic motto: "Democratic

and Fearless; Devoted to No Clique, and Bound to No Master."
Lippard praised the "saucy, independent, fearless, devil-may-care
air" of DuSolle's paper, and when his novel *The Quaker City* was
branded as a scandalous distortion of truth he pointed to the
"City News" section of the *Public Ledger* as proof of the "suicides,
murders, outrages of every sort, now going on, day after day, in
this great city."[8] Lippard's city novels are full of references to the
penny press; indeed, the entire background action of *Memoirs of
a Preacher* and the denouement of *The Quaker City* is communicated
to the reader through characters' readings of news reports in penny
papers.

Another indigenous source of Lippard's sensationalism, the
nativist novel, was the product of embittered American Protestants who often portrayed Catholic priests as pimps or seducers,
nuns as whores, and convents as baby factories and torture sites.
"The grand staple of these stories," Lippard wrote in 1846, "were
such lively topics as adultery and murder; perjury, sacrilege, and
obscenity, were but the lighter decorations of these narratives,"
which he said were characterized by "a downright honest gross-
ness, a plain-spoken foulness, . . . all that is filthy in fact or
literature."[9] Although Lippard regularly decried nativists, he was
influenced by their fiction, as his own novels are crowded with
lustful priests, secret revelers, and demonic torturers.

Lippard also felt the influence of another kind of American
fiction, the historical war novel, which in the 1820s and 1830s
was dominated by John Neal, Robert Montgomery Bird, and
William Gilmore Simms. In *Seventy-Six; or, Love and Battle* (1822)
Neal anticipated Lippard's Revolutionary legends by a bloody,
patriotic retelling of the Battle of Brandywine, in which initially
timid American soldiers, following the example of a godlike
Washington, are "baptized in blood, and hardened in fire."[10]
Similarly, Bird fashioned central characters—Don Gabriel of
Calavar (1834), Juan Lerma of *The Infidel* (1835), and Nathan
Slaughter of *Nick of the Woods* (1837)—who begin as retiring
pacifists or brooding introverts and in the course of the novel are
toughened by combat. Simms, for whom Lippard reserved special
praise, used the colonial and Revolutionary Carolina wilderness

as a setting for violent skirmishes between Indians or Tories and spirited bands of patriots.

Having surveyed this array of literary influences on Lippard, we should recognize that his sensationalism was more than merely the sum total of the lively themes of other writers. Even if we add to this list Brockden Brown's religious fanatic, crazed sleep-walker, and cholera-ridden city, or Poe's crumbling mansion and rat-infested pit, or Dickens's caricatures, or Victor Hugo's hunch-back, the equation still comes up short. Lippard was not just an expert assimilator and popularizer; to a large degree he was an originator. He can be credited with writing fiction that was uncommonly sensational and that often pressed beyond sensationalism toward psychologically suggestive studies of perverse sexuality, sadistic aggression, animality, and apocalyptic dream vision. Thematically and stylistically Lippard launched an assault on the rational equaled in intensity only, in his day, by Poe.

Sex, Violence, Nightmare

When the *Saturday Evening Post* denounced Lippard for arousing the wanton devil of sensuality that lies sleeping in every human heart, it was voicing both the outrage and the fascination that Lippard's fiction evoked. In a day of tight corsets and all-covering outer garments, Lippard brought female breasts before the public eye. He filled his pages with beautiful women partially or totally *en déshabillé,* though he made sure that nothing more than lips, skin, hair, legs, and "snowy globes" were described. Usually Lippard's descriptions of this half-nakedness were as static as photographs: several of his heroines are reclining languorously on couches with their robes loosened; others are resting in bed with the top sheet pulled partway down; one, a naked slave girl on a trade block, is standing motionless before a crowd of in-quisitive men. Lippard thus appealed to, and in fact may have helped to create, a uniquely American kind of voyeurism that has been widely exploited in the twentieth century.

Sex in Lippard's fiction is lascivious and teasing rather than pornographic or explicit. An exasperating master of literary *coitus interruptus,* Lippard regularly carries his characters to the brink of sexual consummation and then coyly withdraws, leaving his puritanical readers shocked that he has gone so far and his prurient ones panting for more. Lippard's treatment of sex raises a fundamental question about his mission as a novelist: was he, as his critics charged, writing salacious fiction, or was he, as he and his friends claimed, presenting sex only to punish it? Was *The Quaker City* indeed "the most immoral work of the age," or was it, in Lippard's words, "destitute of any idea of sensualism"?[11]

We cannot doubt that Lippard was in part determined to protest against illicit sex. As a journalist for the *Citizen Soldier* in April 1843 he editorially applauded the acquittal of Singleton Mercer for the murder of his sister's seducer, and after that he campaigned for stricter antiseduction laws in Pennsylvania. He then wrote *The Quaker City* to show, in his words, *"that the seduction of a poor and innocent girl, is a deed altogether as criminal as deliberate murder. It is worse than murder of the body, for it is the assassination of the soul"* (*The Quaker City*, p. [1]). This attitude, almost a caricature of Victorian prudishness, was visible in the main plot of *The Quaker City*, as Lippard portrayed Byrnewood Arlington tracking down and finally killing Gus Lorrimer, the heartless youth who had seduced Byrnewood's sister in Monk Hall. It was equally evident in *Memoirs of a Preacher*, in which Charles Lester wreaks vengeance upon Edmund Jervis, the popular preacher who had ruined Lester's sister by marrying and then abandoning her. Indeed, nearly every Lippard novel contains at least one plot involving a female victimized by a rake who is punished in the end.

Beneath this moral surface, however, lay an undeniable fascination with sin and perversion that carried Lippard beyond the Richardsonian or penny-dreadful tradition. Often Lippard's reformist aim to unveil hidden corruption and his journalistic one to report anything lively combined to create a hypnotic involvement with the debauchery he ostensibly lamented. As a result, Lippard conjured up some of the most perverse situations in nineteenth-century American fiction.

Lippard's underlying attraction to the theme of sexual aberration can be suggested initially by the ways he revised the Heberton-Mercer affair to make it more violent and ironic. In actuality, the wealthy bachelor Mahlon Heberton, after boasting to his oyster-cellar companions of his nefarious designs, lured the unsuspecting Sarah Mercer into the house of a Philadelphia mulatto woman, where he seduced her on a promise of marriage. A few days later, fearing reprisal from Sarah's brother Singleton, Mahlon boarded a Camden-bound ferry on which he was shot by Singleton while sitting quietly in his coach. In Lippard's embellished version of the story, one of the oyster-cellar companions to whom Gus Lorrimer (Mahlon Heberton) boasts is Byrnewood Arlington (Singleton Mercer), who playfully bets that Gus cannot seduce a certain virgin and who turns against Gus only when he discovers that the virgin in question is his own sister. The irony deepens when we learn that Byrnewood in his own right has seduced and abandoned a young woman, and that his sister Mary, quite unlike the rather dim-witted Sarah Mercer, slyly schemes to meet Gus, then continues to love him madly even after he has deflowered her. Also, Lippard transforms the mulatto woman's house into the mammoth Monk Hall, run by various grotesque pimps and procuresses who oversee many seductions going on simultaneously. Instead of the mere promise of marriage made by Heberton, Lippard gives us a sham wedding ceremony conducted by Lorrimer's friends, followed by a night of nuptial bliss that leads to Mary's undying, crazed infatuation for Lorrimer. Byrnewood Arlington's revenge is not a quick gunshot on a crowded ferry; rather, it is a prolonged confrontation on a small fishing boat in which Byrnewood shoots Lorrimer after denouncing him and then has a sanguinary fantasy of drinking the libertine's blood and dancing on his corpse.

Lippard has transformed a relatively uncomplicated case of seduction and revenge into a fictional plot in which not only the seducer but also the virgin and her brother exhibit various degrees of hypocrisy, masochism, sadism, or incestuous devotion. This exaggeration of the perverse is even more apparent in other sexual scenes in *The Quaker City*. In one the lustful preacher F. A. T. Pyne administers a love potion to a young woman, Mabel, who he mistakenly thinks is his long-lost daughter. In another the cuckold Albert Livingstone sneaks into Monk Hall, where he sees his wife, Dora, lying naked beside her lover, Algernon Fitz-Cowles; from the sleeping lovers Livingstone snips lockets of hair that he later presents to his wife, whose shocked agony increases when he poisons her as her coffin is brought into their mansion. The Livingstone plot is made even more perverse by the machinations of Luke Harvey, Dora's ex-lover, who at first warns Livingstone of his wife's adultery but later comes close to demanding sexual favors of Dora in return for a promise of future silence.

Such sexual bribery is common practice in Monk Hall, where clergymen, lawyers, editors, and businessmen—Philadelphia's evil "monks"—convene nightly to wine, dine, and consummate seductions under the supervision of Devil-Bug and his demonic helpers. Devil-Bug is the book's most monstrous embodiment of the perverse, as he not only arranges many illicit liaisons but also leers lustfully at several imperiled women, even one he helps to rescue. And the women themselves are neither the innocent victims of the British penny dreadful nor the pure flowers of the American domestic novel. Dora Livingstone is a complex amalgam of venality, independence, duplicity, intellect, and raw sensuality. Even the comparatively virtuous Mary and Mabel become physically aroused in ways that belie their ostensible naiveté.

Thus, nearly every character in *The Quaker City* becomes trapped in the sexual labyrinth Lippard has created. This also occurs in several other Lippard novels. In *Blanche of Brandywine* (1846) one woman is raped by British soldiers, another is trapped in a cave with a brutish American, and a third poisons herself after seeing her fiancé fondling another woman. The hero of *Paul Ardenheim* (1848) is diverted from patriotic and filial duty by a voluptuous demon-woman who lures him into her bedroom. *The Empire City* (1849) and *New York* (1853) describe or suggest nearly every variety of illicit sexual behavior—prostitution, adultery, necrophilia, homosexuality, miscegenation, the seduction of slaves and adolescents. In one memorable scene in *The Empire City* the Rev. Herman Barnhurst whispers lecherously to a teen-aged boy sitting next to him on a train; the boy, we soon learn, is the disguised

Alice Burney, whose father is standing in the aisle nearby unaware that his daughter is being seduced before his eyes. In *New York* Lippard describes a situation—one that has been called "one of the most grotesque combinations of sex and death in literature"[12]— in which a woman sweetly inveigles her paramour to her "bridal bed," where she has hidden the moldering corpse of her murdered husband as a horrific reminder of the paramour's sins.

In short, if Lippard was opposed to seduction, he was even more violently opposed to the hypocrisy he saw all around him, and he was ready to explore uncharted areas of sexuality in order to shock his readers out of their sanctimonious respectability. The ferocity of his reformist purpose drove him to fashion fictional situations that in their perversity cracked the brittle shell of American middle-class morality.

With the eye of a true penny-press reporter, Lippard fastened on actual instances of corruption that seemed to validate the perverse themes of his fiction. For example, he devoted several trenchant passages in essays and in fiction to the notorious case of Benjamin T. Onderdonk, the Anglican bishop of New York who in 1844 was brought to trial on charges of seducing several of his parishioners' wives and was defrocked the next year. In 1845 the Onderdonk trial proceedings, more than two hundred pages of cross-examination in which Onderdonk's victims described in detail the bishop's sexual advances, were published in pamphlet form, enjoying a quick and widespread sale. In Lippard's eyes, everyone involved in the Onderdonk affair was at fault: the bishop was "a wine-bibber, a sensualist, an adulterer," his accusers were "as base calumniators as ever disgraced the earth," and the trial pamphlet was "stained with the pollution of lascivious deeds."[13]

If Lippard saw in the Onderdonk case proof of preachers' profligacy and publishers' exploitation, in the life of the editor and anthologist Rufus Wilmot Griswold he found evidence of bogus morality. Griswold had married a southern woman in the belief that she was wealthy and then left her when he discovered she was not. He then published a pamphlet about the divorce in which he charged his former wife with trying to hoodwink him;

subsequently the woman nearly went insane with grief. Lippard, in a digressive passage in his novel *'Bel of Prairie Eden* (1848), wrote that the "moral editor of a Moral Newspaper" was driven by "impulses . . . like the bubble of the Dead Sea, stagnant and pestilent excretions fomenting on the very dregs of rottenness and decay." To prove this Lippard pointed to "the victim of this *chaste* editor's perjury—a broken-hearted and wronged woman" who "lay mad and howling in the cell of an insane asylum."[14]

Lippard's response to the Onderdonk, Griswold, and Heberton-Mercer affairs, as well as the emphasis on sexual perversity in his fiction, might suggest that he was a sensation-monger who wrote on racy topics merely to gain attention, stir up trouble, or make money. In reality, Lippard rarely evidenced the sheer opportunistic sensationalism of several of the American "city mysteries" novelists of the period, particularly George Foster, Henri Foster, and George Thompson. Such novels as Thompson's *City Crimes* (1849) and Henri Foster's *Ellen Grafton* (1850) descended to the level of bald thrillsmanship and monotonous prurience in a way that Lippard's fiction never did. These city novelists tried to outdo each other in pornographic excess; Thompson, for instance, takes us into a squalid cavern below New York's Five Points district, where "the crime of *incest* is as common . . . as dirt. I have known a mother and her son—a father and his daughter—a brother and sister—to be guilty of criminal intimacy!"[15] The competitive spirit of the sensationalists is apparent in an anonymous novelist's claim: "There are those who pretend that Philadelphia and Boston are ahead of New York in the race of profligacy. My own opinion is, that it seems worse in those places, simply on account of their pretensions to superior propriety and piety."[16]

At his best, Lippard avoided this shoddy competition by straining not only to reproduce the beauties and the dangers of sexual passion but also to translate sex into psychological and symbolic terms. In his description of Monk Hall, with its trap doors always threatening to spring open and send one hurtling several stories down into rat-infested caverns, Lippard redirects the familiar device of a structure representing the mind toward a pre-Freudian symbol of the human psyche, with the id lurking darkly below surface consciousness. If Lippard never shows the sex act, he does try to capture the warm glow of sexual excitement. At one point in *The Quaker City* we see Mabel, who has swallowed an aphrodisiac that has "aroused her animal nature," feeling her body relax into "the flowing outlines of voluptuous beauty" and her face growing "radiant with passion."[17] In another scene, Dora, "a perfect incarnation of the Sensual Woman," lies next to her lover as her "thick masses of jet-black hair fell, glossy and luxuriant, over her round neck and along her uncovered bosom, which swelling with the full ripeness of womanhood, rose gently in the light" (117). Several times in *The Quaker City* Lippard stresses that woman, like man, has animalistic impulses that are at once frighteningly destructive and richly alluring.

This paradoxical recognition of the terror and wonder of sexuality surfaces in his portrayal of the priest-wizard Ravoni at the end of the novel. Ravoni is a picture of physical excess, presenting for public inspection the naked body of an unconscious woman and surrounding himself with fawning priestesses who circle around him in transparent gowns amidst wreaths of incense. Lippard is obviously drawn to these hedonistic rituals and to Ravoni's credo: " 'I will teach men that in the Refined cultivation of the Senses is Happiness. Not a pore on the body but may be made the Minister of some new Joy; not a throb in the veins, but may become a living Pleasure' " (359).

While Lippard brought to American fiction a flexible comprehension of sexuality, he was even bolder in his studies of violence and gore. In *The Ladye Annabel* (1843–1844) he multiplied and exaggerated Gothic devices to create vivid scenes of torture, live burial, and rotting corpses. In his historical legends, ranging from *Herbert Tracy* (1842) to *Washington and His Generals* and *Legends of Mexico* (both 1847), he transferred blood and savagery from the medieval castle to the American battlefield, becoming one of a handful of antebellum American novelists who described the terrors of war with some amount of realism. In his several urban novels he summoned brute violence into the heart of the modern city. Toward the end of his life, in *Adonai: The*

Pilgrim of Eternity (1851), he pressed beyond such graphic horror toward an all-consuming vision of cynicism.

The Ladye Annabel, a novel about political intrigue and revolution in medieval Florence, is most interesting to twentieth-century readers for its scenes of grisly sadism verging on black humor, scenes that seem to enact Lippard's statement: "In the breast of the man to whom God has given a soul, there also dwells at all times a demon; and that demon arises into fearful action from the ruins of betrayed confidence."[18] The book is full of lip-smacking accounts of decomposing corpses, spurting blood, and quivering torsos during torture. The Doomsman, a mad executioner who hovers in and out of the action, at one point has a "merry fancy" of punishing a criminal on the rack: the victim's bones crack and tear through the skin as the rack tightens; the victim writhes and screams as the Doomsman scoops out the eyeballs and pours molten lead into the sockets; then the Doomsman breaks open the chest with a jagged club, rips out the victim's heart, and holds it "still quivering on high" as the "warm blood-drops fall pattering on the face of the felon" (51). The main character of the novel, a fiendish sorcerer named Aldarin who drugs and strangles his royal brother in an attempt to gain control of Florence, is similarly surrounded with images of gory violence. In the Red Chamber, where he performs alchemical experiments, Aldarin stores "lifeless trunks, all hewn and hacked," with "discolored faces, green with decay; with the eyes scooped from the sockets, the livid skin dropping from the forehead, . . . and the brain, once the resting place of the mighty soul, protruding in all its discoloration and corruption over the bared brow" (40). Aldarin himself meets a gruesome end, as his execution by vivisection leaves only "a limbless trunk" lying "in the dust of the highway, spouting streams of blood" (184).

All this might be dismissed as sheer Gothic excess were it not linked to a more metaphysical preoccupation with mortality and negativity. What Poe called the "richly inventive and imaginative" quality of *The Ladye Annabel* is especially apparent in moments when descriptions of physical decay lead Lippard to harrowing contemplation of life's transience. Such contemplation concludes the account of the corpses in the Red Chamber, as Lippard describes "these ghastly remains of humanity, these fearful mockeries of life, these rotting relics of what had once enthroned the GIANT SOUL" (40). It appears even more vividly in several dreams of the afterlife that occur in the novel. At the moment when Aldarin believes his political schemes are succeeding, he has a nightmare of floating in the fiery ocean of hell with "the bodies of the lost, offensive with decay . . . throwing their crumbling arms around his neck and fixing their livid lips upon his burning cheek, in the kiss of the damned" (43). Even the virtuous hero of the novel, Adrian, is besieged by terrifying visions. In one, Adrian envisions two successive scenes: a huge dance hall filled with beautifully dressed Florentines whirling to festive music; and, a hundred years later, the same people reappearing as clothed skeletons, being drawn to the hall in caskets, and emerging to dance in a clattering revelry of death. Interpreting this "dance of woe" as "a ghastly mimicry of life, reality and joy," Adrian gloomily generalizes: "To-day the children of men live and love, hate and destroy. Where are their lives, their loves, their hatreds, and their wars, in an hundred years?" (238).

This brooding recognition of the larger implications of physical decay carried over into Lippard's war novels. Lippard's patriotic respect for sterling soldiership was qualified by an acute perception of the grisly realities of the battlefield. In his accounts of Revolutionary or Mexican War combat Lippard frequently begins by highlighting the heroism of American soldiers and ends by describing the bloody aftermath of battle. Anticipating such later war novelists as John W. De Forest, Stephen Crane, and Ernest Hemingway, Lippard allowed his enthusiasm over man's bravery to dissolve periodically into an ironic recognition of war's inhumanity, shifting rapidly from heady jingoism to a kind of grim naturalism. For example, after describing Americans' heroism in the Battle of Brandywine, he shifts the mood in his account of the battle's outcome: "There were senseless carcasses, with the arms rent from the shattered body, . . . with foreheads severed by the sword thrust, with hair dabbled in blood, with sunken jaws fallen on the gory chest; there was all the horror, all the bloodshed, all the butchery of war, without a single gleam of its romance or chivalry."[19]

While Lippard viewed preparation for battle as joyfully heroic and the aftermath as often coldly depressing, he saw the battle itself as a kind of watershed moment when joy and gloom commingled and when man was exhilaratingly free to vent his most savage impulses. His most memorable battle scenes remove the reader to a netherworld where violence and brutality reign. One of his most popular Revolutionary legends concerned a band of five patriots—a herculean Negro, a hunter, a blacksmith, and two farmers—who slashed their way through Tory lines not with bayonets or rifles but with hammers, axes, sickles, and clubs. This story of the Oath-Bound Five at Brandywine had powerful mass appeal both because of its egalitarian overtones and its suggestions of unbridled atavistic impulses. While describing the Oath-Bound Five in the heat of battle, Lippard wrote an unusual and forceful dark passage:

Dark and mysterious are the instincts of man, dark and foul is that instinct of lust, which grapples with womanly beauty, like a beast gorging his bleeding food; dark and dread is that instinct of Hunger, which has put such fire in a Mother's veins, such agony in her heart, that she has devoured her own babe, tearing it to gory fragments as it hung smiling on her wasted bosom; dark and horrible is that instinct of Life, which makes a man forget honor, forswear his own father, and give his dearest friend to death, in order that he, may prolong a few hours of ignominious existence; but darker and . . . most horrible of all, is the instinct of Carnage! Yes, that Instinct which makes a man thirst for blood, which makes him mad with joy, when he steeps his arms to the elbows in his foeman's gore, which makes him shout and halloo, and laugh, as he goes murdering on over piles of dead![20]

In such passages Lippard became pre-Modern in a way that more familiar writers of the American Renaissance usually did not. He pointed beyond Poe's psychological terror or Melville's ambiguities or Hawthorne's gloom toward the bestiality and perversity evident in some avant-garde fiction of the twentieth century. If French surrealists of the 1920s admired the eighteenth-century Gothic novelists and such a nineteenth-century iconoclast as Comte de Lautréamont for their violent rejection of rational order and social morality, they would have appreciated those moments in Lippard's fiction when sober reason is fiercely stripped away, when Lippard gleefully hurls the reader into the teeming Pandora's box of the subconscious.[21]

Lippard's assault on the rational manifests itself in various ways. It appears most obviously in the grotesque animal characters that abound in his fiction. One of Lippard's contemporaries was shocked by Lippard's tendency to represent man as a "human giraffe, or a ghoul, or some other . . . creature whom everybody hates and nobody has ever seen."[22] This tendency was apparent in Lippard's writing from the beginning. As Billy Brier in the *Spirit of the Times* he described a newspaper editor who combined the features of a bull terrier, a cat, an ape, and a lap dog.[23] In "The Spermaceti Papers" in the *Citizen Soldier* he compared a magazine publisher to a weasel, a pig, and a maggot to show how "the spirits of animals enter the bodies of men."[24] In *Blanche of Brandywine* he not only links several characters to vultures, ravens, and spiders but also portrays two "twin shapes of grotesque ugliness," Blood and Death, whose sole delight as battlefield scavengers is to "revel amid scenes of corruption and blood."[25] The hideous Malachi Ham of *The Nazarene* is described as half man and half beast, the dwarfish hunchback Black David of *Paul Ardenheim* has a horselike face, and other Lippard characters are associated with animals through such names as Buzby Poodle, Calvin Wolfe, and Bloodhound.

Lippard's most fully developed animal characters are Devil-Bug, Musquito, and Glow-worm, the keepers of Monk Hall in *The Quaker City*. A one-eyed monster with bristling teeth and long hairy arms, Devil-Bug is "a wild beast, a snake, a reptile, or a devil incarnate—any thing but—a man."[26] His helpers are "additional insects, . . . singular specimens of the glow-worm and musquito" (45). These grotesque figures epitomize the immorality and amorality that Lippard sees seething below the staid surface of the Quaker City. They ply their guests with opium and brandy, dash out the brains of old ladies, spring trap doors, and tote unconscious people into their underground cavern. Before Lautréamont, Kafka, or William S. Burroughs, Lippard was grafting together the human and the animalistic or subhuman to mock moral certainty and puncture pious pretensions.

Another antirational device Lippard uses is what may be called in the broadest sense dream imagery but which includes not only sleeping and waking visions but also drug-induced states and magnetic or clairvoyant trances. In his employment of dream imagery Lippard again presaged twentieth-century surrealists, who believe, in André Breton's words, "in the omnipotence of dream and in the disinterested play of thought," or, in Georges Hugnet's, in the capacity of dream to "tear up the real."[27] Lippard regularly uses dreams and trances to break away from chronological time and limitations of space, to permit irrational fears and fantasies to surface, and to distort common reality.

We have seen how Aldarin and Adrian of *The Ladye Annabel* have gruesome visions of the afterlife. In *The Quaker City* Lippard creates an entire nightmare world that is always threatening to destroy ordinary perceptions of objective surroundings. In the first chapter we see, through the eyes of the drunken Gus Lorrimer, the lamp-posts and sidewalks of Philadelphia perform dizzying pirouettes in the air. This is a confused and confusing city, in Gus's words, with " 'every thing fleeting and nothing stable, every thing shifting and changing, and nothing substantial,' " a city where "a mass of miserable frame houses [seem] about to commit suicide and fling themselves madly into the gutter." Distant factories and office buildings are "looming in broken perspective" and looking "as if they wanted to shake hands across the narrow street."[28]

The most nightmarish place in the city is Monk Hall, where outwardly normal folk become "entangled in the mazes of some hideous dream" (64). In the main hall, revelers are "fast advancing to that state of brutal inebriety, when strange-looking stars shine in the place of lamps, when the bottles dance and even the tables perform the cracovienne, while all sorts of beehives create a buzzing murmur in the air" (48). Upstairs the ruined Mary Arlington is envisaging "a chaos of ashes, and mouldering flame; a lurid sky above, a blasted soil below, and one immense horizon of leaden clouds, hemming in the universe of desolation" (124). In the underground cavern Devil-Bug has an apocalyptic dream of "The Last Day of the Quaker City." At first he is "surrounded by a hazy atmosphere, with coffins floating slowly past, and the stars shining through the eyes of skulls, and the sun pouring his livid light straight downward into a wilderness of new-made graves, which extended yawning and dismal over the surface of a boundless plain" (313). The vision becomes even stranger when he sees Philadelphia in 1950, with coffin fleets battling on the Schuylkill River, shadowy specters peering over the shoulders of preachers and businessmen, people whirling through the air, and then the whole scene exploding into a chaos of destruction as the sky is illuminated by the flaming words, "WO UNTO SODOM!"

Lippard continued to experiment with dream imagery in his later fiction. The heroine of *Memoirs of a Preacher* is put into a magnetic trance in which her mind wanders freely into the past and future and into the afterlife as well. Hypnotized characters in *Paul Ardenheim* and *The Empire City* have the power, respectively, to see through thick walls and to admire a woman's body through her clothing. The first-person narrator of a story in *The Midnight Queen* describes how in a long period of insanity he saw a "grotesque and nightmare panorama" in which his soul flew to a barren planet millions of miles away and then returned to earth to take on the shapes, in rapid succession, of a putrescent corpse, a howling "inferior animal," a bloodthirsty Napoleon in battle, and an old hag strung up by a noose but never dying. "Dream succeeded dream," the narrator says, "not like the visions of a fever, but most strangely and horribly palpable; and I had no existence of my own."[29] It is this kind of total surrender of the ego to a free-floating dream world that modern surrealists have valued so highly. Lippard's intentional distortion of objective reality places him in a small group of pre-1900 writers—including, in America, Brockden Brown and Poe—who heightened attacks on conventional values with reproductions of irrational states.

The Style of the Irrational

Lippard's exploration of sex, violence, and dream was facilitated by his use of stylistic devices that departed markedly from novelistic norms of his time. Lippard brashly violated narrative linearity and chronological sequence and at the same time shifted tone and perspective to create a kind of quicksand effect. The reader of a Lippard novel is rarely allowed to enjoy the security of a predictable plot or a consistent authorial voice. In a curious way, the typical Lippard novel is like Monk Hall, a labyrinthine structure riddled with trap doors that are always opening beneath the reader's feet and sending him tumbling into another dimension. And Lippard is like an ever-present Devil-Bug, sometimes preaching, sometimes praying, sometimes rescuing the poor or virtuous, yet always ready to gloat fiendishly over a decayed corpse or an old woman's brains splattered on the floor.

Until quite recently it was generally believed that Lippard was merely an undisciplined writer who had no control over his plot and characters. In his own day Lippard's critics charged him with a lack of classical restraint, a disrespect for rules of syntax and grammar, and a feverish emotionalism bordering on insanity. Even his friend Chauncey Burr wrote rather apologetically of *The Quaker City:* "We may overlook its zigzag, fragmentary, *quasi*-chaotic manner of saying some things, since it utters so many other things with such surpassing strength and beauty."[30] In the twentieth century Lippard's plots have sometimes been called tangled series of adventurous episodes, his characters colorful but shallow puppets, his invective rant. Although since 1970 several critics have argued persuasively against this almost uniformly negative assessment, no one has studied Lippard's style with any precision or recognized that in certain senses it was just as bold and original as his ideas.

While thematically Lippard was manipulating previous types of popular literature to make innovative combinations, stylistically he was doing the same. His seemingly chaotic plot arrangement was an exaggeration of what has been aptly described as the "centrifugal" structure of the *roman-feuilleton.*[31] Unlike more traditional novelists, writers of the *roman-feuilleton* rarely carried one or two tightly controlled plots to a single climax followed by a denouement. In order to answer popular demand for constant suspense and entertainment, they usually brought each serial installment to a climax of its own, always leaving readers on the brink of some disaster or consummation. When the serial segments were gathered together and published as a single volume, the narrative as a whole had a kind of roller-coaster effect, rising to a climax, falling off precipitously, and then rising and falling again in a seemingly endless succession of peaks and valleys, dips and curves.

Lippard's contribution to this style was a conscious acceleration of centrifugal devices to break down unities of time and space. In the epilogue to *Paul Ardenheim* Lippard complained that American fiction "of the present day, does not present extravagant views of life, or paint pictures that transcend probability; its delineations, on the contrary, are only extravagant in their tameness, and transcendent in their mathematical probability." The plot of *Paul Ardenheim,* he writes, is "utterly impossible" and "altogether improbable"; "the author . . . prides himself on having written *'the most improbable book in the world.' "*[32] Similarly, he claimed that *The Nazarene* was "strange," at variance with the "rules of critics," and unlike anything ever published in America.[33]

Lippard acted upon such boasts by determinedly contravening normal standards of plot development and chronology. The French writers of the *roman-feuilleton* were almost always linear and chronological within each serial segment, and in most cases they sustained a forward-moving direction in successive installments. Lippard, in contrast, regularly shifted to a different time and place at the beginning of each chapter, not to mention the even more marked shifts he made between segments. His assault on the rational was thus stylistically enforced by a dreamlike hovering between events and characters often related in no other way than a shared improbability or freakishness. One thinks again of the surrealists, who prize in a writer such as Lautréamont precisely those qualities that official criticism rejects: studied disruptions of narrative sequence; puppetlike characters largely

devoid of psychological motivation; an atmosphere of violence
and perversity; and an overall rebellion against comforting consequentiality and exact verisimilitude.[34]

These qualities, pervasive in Lippard's fiction, are especially
evident in Part Two of *The Empire City*. The section begins with
an unknown man placing a huge log on a railroad track with the
aim of derailing the onrushing "steam-devil," compared by Lippard to the nineteenth century "hurled by its own mad impulses"
and crushing "the weak . . . with a shriek, and bathing its iron
wheels in their blood."[35] The train is only two yards away from
the log, with the engineer sticking his head frantically out the
window, when Lippard ends the chapter.

This is normal *roman-feuilleton* procedure, but what comes next
is not. Instead of observing the expected pattern by beginning
the next chapter with the crash, followed by the dispersal of the
survivors from the wreck, Lippard abruptly pulls the reader a half
an hour back in time to a scene in the train's baggage car, where
an ex-convict and a suicidal vagabond are lamenting their miserable plights. Then Lippard carries the reader even further back
in time to witness successive strange scenes in separate passenger
cars: a Trinity Church minister seducing a young girl in boys'
clothing; an unctuous statesman promising to protect a runaway
slave woman he secretly plans to ravish; a bank president who
boasts to a policeman of his schemes to cheat the poor but whose
money-filled valise is being stolen as he speaks; a South Carolina
slave-hunter talking of two runaways he is trying to track down,
unaware that they are sitting nearby. Chronology is even more
violently disrupted when Lippard has one of the slaves fall off the
train, which stops, backs up for more than a mile, and waits
while several passengers disembark to search for the body. Once
the train gets rolling again Lippard resumes his narrative leaps
from one car to another to trace the attempted suicides, seductions, and robberies occurring simultaneously. Just as the reader
is tensely wondering about the log on the track, Lippard shifts
the scene to the dark woods, where he describes a deafening crash
and the train "like the dragon of some old-time fable, at first
madly endeavoring to tear its antagonist with its teeth, and then

leaping into the air, with volumes of smoke and flame streaming from its expanded jaws" until it collapses to the ground (100).

In reading this section, we often feel the bewilderment of one of the train passengers who confesses to feeling trapped in "a dream," a "hideous nightmare" (75). In effect, Lippard has the reader, along with the train, rushing forward and backward at the same time. We might be able to dismiss this device as clumsy craftsmanship were it not for the fact that thematically the section is quite unified and that our disorientation is a main ingredient of the effect Lippard is trying to create. Lippard has converted the railroad train, a proud symbol of nineteenth-century technological order and progress, into a fierce monster crushing "the weak" as it roars madly on. In the bowels of this huge monster are other outwardly rational monsters (a clergyman, a politician, a bank president, a slave-catcher, a policeman) who in various ways are victimizing the weak (a homeless girl, the poor, runaway slaves). This is indeed a "hideous nightmare" in which savagery lies below civilized surfaces, and the truest way to duplicate nightmare is to break down normal patterns of time and space. The section is far more effective as it stands than it would have been had Lippard, say, begun with the train several miles away from the log and then described sequentially the goings on in the various cars. When the train rears up and topples over at the end, we are tempted to applaud Lippard as a literary St. George who has used the sharp sword of alinear style to slay the dragon of rationality.

Nearly every Lippard novel underscores theme with experimental stylistic devices in this way. In *The Nazarene* the cruelty of nineteenth-century nativists and capitalists is linked to historical examples of bloodthirstiness through time leaps backward to early-Christian and medieval times. In *Paul Ardenheim* and *Washington and His Generals* Lippard connects the American Revolution to previous poor men's revolutions and associations by recreating scenes about the lowly Carpenter of Nazareth and the fifteenth-century Brotherhood of the Rosy Cross.

Adonai: The Pilgrim of Eternity is perhaps Lippard's boldest attempt to jettison the restrictions of rational probability. In this work Lippard has an early-Roman convert to Christianity travel from third-century Rome to Germany during the Reformation and then on to various scenes in nineteenth-century Europe and America. Along the way this pilgrim, Adonai, is joined by the soul of George Washington; both are accompanied by the Executioner, an omnipresent spirit of evil who sneers at their dreams of social reform and universal progress. Lippard juggles allegorical and realistic modes to escape conventional narrative patterns, as the wanderers drift freely through time and space, by turns conversing with actual people in different countries, traveling into the afterlife, and having mountain-top visions of the past and future. In his characterization of the Executioner—who in some ways presages Dostoevski's Grand Inquisitor or Mark Twain's Mysterious Stranger—Lippard exaggerates the gloom of his previous portraits of Gothic horror while leaving behind the gore and violence. Calling progress a lie, the Executioner predicts that divisions over the issue of slavery will lead to terrible civil war and that the industrial machines man has created will eventually destroy him. Although at the end of the novel the appearance of a poor wayfarer carrying a cross makes the Executioner disappear, an underlying sense of impending tragedy and doom pervades the book, and we feel that in the Executioner Lippard has at last discovered a full expression of the negativity implicit in several of his earlier works.

In sum, in various kinds of fiction—Gothic and contemporary, sensational and metaphysical, patriotic and reformist—Lippard combined thematic attacks on civilized respectability and staid rationality with a style that was consciously disruptive, quirky, and disrespectful of linear patterns. Stylistically, the kinds of spatial and temporal disunities Lippard was experimenting with would be developed in more cerebral, self-conscious fashion by such later writers as Faulkner, Joyce, Virginia Woolf, and Nabokov. For Lippard, whose credo was "have something to say, and say it with all your might," these disunities were the product of a volcanic imagination spewing forth hot rage against the social and literary establishment.[36]

Chapter Three

Reactionary Radicalism: Lippard's Treatment of Society and History

Having written extended urban exposé fiction, founded a labor organization, and fabricated patriotic myths of long-lasting cultural significance, Lippard has been justly praised for his innovative social and political views. These views were a unique blend of backward-looking and forward-looking tendencies, a reactionary radicalism that held up early Christianity, medieval ritualistic associations, and the American Revolution as models for the labor reform Lippard thought was needed to eliminate the cruel inequities and capitalist exploitation he saw everywhere in urban America. The redirection of tested literary modes evident in Lippard's sensationalism was duplicated in his treatment of society by a canny manipulation of seemingly incongruous historical currents and of volatile public opinion. While Lippard's urban fiction aroused the ire and pricked the conscience of city dwellers, his historical fiction mythologized the early-Christian and American past so convincingly that his fanciful legends were accepted as fact by thousands of Americans.

The City and Current Social Issues in Lippard's Fiction

"There is a Curse upon the great city," Lippard writes in *The Man with the Mask* (1849). "With the lowly poor in their dens of want, in the narrow alleys where squalid crime drowns the fever of despair in draughts of liquid fire, and in the great man-

sion, where the revel, bought with the poor man's labor, roars
on from midnight until the break of day."[1]

The city in Lippard's fiction is usually not the coldly banal,
depressingly quotidian city of late-nineteenth-century naturalistic
novels; rather, it is a mysterious jungle, comparable in mythic
proportions to Cooper's wilderness or Melville's sea, full of hidden
horrors and savage struggles at once appalling and fascinating to
Lippard. In his treatment of the city Lippard created a kind of
halfway house between "Monk" Lewis and Theodore Dreiser, a
place where Gothic terror was politicized and made frighteningly
contemporary.

Images of this new urban Gothic abound in Lippard's fiction.
Lippard transforms the medieval monks of the Gothic novel into
modern monks—wealthy or aristocratic Philadelphians and New
Yorkers outwardly moral but secretly devoted to sensualism and
vice. The sites of their debauchery—Monk Hall in *The Quaker
City,* Caleb Goodleigh's mansion in *Memoirs of a Preacher,* the
Temple and Madame Resimer's whorehouse in *New York*—are
updated versions of the Gothic castle, towering structures of
uncertain dimensions and mythical origins in which hypocritical
sanctity is stripped away to expose the lust and violence beneath
surface virtue. The city surrounding these structures is also imbued with Gothic atmosphere. The streets are not those monot-
onously straight American avenues that bored the visiting Charles
Dickens in 1842; instead, they are "streets dark as grave-vaults,
and laid out in old times, with a profound contempt of right
angles—streets walled in with huge warehouses, above whose
lofty roofs, you caught but a glimpse of the midnight stars."[2]
Wandering through this maze, Lippard's characters often glimpse
other urban Gothic scenes, such as the Bank of the United States
glistening in the moonlight like a "sepulchre of dead fortunes,"[3]
or Trinity Church looming like "a huge Gothic pile, whose foundation is among the graves, and whose unfinished spire already
seems to touch the stars,"[4] or a gaunt person drifting through
the glittering crowds of Broadway "like a specter through the
mazes of a voluptuous dance,"[5] or a starving seamstress gripped
by "the Skeleton Hand of Poverty."[6]

While Lippard exploited bygone Gothicism for its suggestions of supernaturalism and grotesquerie, he occasionally pointed toward the stark verisimilitude of the realists and naturalists. In *Memoirs of a Preacher* he interrupts a description of an indigent Philadelphia family to comment: "You will observe once for all, that we have set out in our task with the intention to paint human beings. We have nothing to do with heroes or heroines. We have not time for that kind of thing. So much Reality lies along our path—Reality, vivid and appalling—Reality as palpable as is the corpse whose very touch chills you from the hand to the heart—that we have no time and not much inclination for Fiction."[7] This statement epitomizes Lippard's two-sided position as a city novelist: on one hand, his dismissal of "heroes or heroines" and "Fiction" represents a protest against prettified romanticism, prefiguring the urban realism of Howells and Dreiser; on the other hand, the "Reality" Lippard embraces is not Howells's cult of the commonplace but rather the "vivid and appalling," corpselike reality of the Gothic fictionists. Unlike the Gothicists of the past, Lippard was able to direct penny-press and *roman-feuilleton* urban reportage toward prophetic descriptions of the new locus of horror, the nineteenth-century city, with its dens of vice and crowded tenements. Unlike the realists of the future, he could invoke Gothic convention for its monster figures, labyrinthine structures, and supernatural occurrences. The resultant combination was an unusual brand of urban fiction that was by turns realistic and surrealistic, topically political and improbably sensational, clear-eyed in its social commentary and bold in its probings of irrational states.

A controlling theme of Lippard's urban fiction is that superficially respectable types are in fact ogres whose callous indifference to the poor is equalled only by their private venality and licentiousness. One of Lippard's favorite targets was the Protestant preacher, usually portrayed as a bigoted nativist who organizes tract societies to save heathen abroad while ignoring the poor at home. Such clergymen characters as F. A. T. Pyne, Herman Barnhurst, and Edmund Jervis apply the money they earn from hellfire preaching toward the purchase of drugs and alcohol, the seduction of young women, or both.

Other elite figures Lippard satirized were bank directors, landlords, politicians, and newspaper editors. Lippard's animus against bank directors sprung from the closure of several Philadelphia banks between 1837 and 1842. Like many other democratically inclined Americans of his time, Lippard thought that such bank directors as Nicholas Biddle were conspiring to defraud the poor of their hard-earned savings. Lippard created several fictional scenes that illustrated this idea. In a vignette toward the end of *The Quaker City* he describes an indigent laborer, John Davis, trying to extract a small sum he has deposited in the bank of Job Joneson, "one of your good citizens, who subscribe large sums to tract societies, and sport velvet-cushioned pews in the church."[8] After Joneson refuses to return Davis's savings because the bank has failed, Davis returns home to find his wife and daughter dead of starvation, at which point the poor man commits suicide. Israel Yorke of *The Empire City* intentionally creates a run on his several banks so that he can cheat the poor out of their savings and buy up their notes at a cheap price. Equally villainous bank directors in Lippard's fiction are Calvin Wolfe of *The Nazarene,* Jacob Hicks of *The Killers,* and Ewen MacGregor of *'Bel of Prairie Eden.* Of these characters Calvin Wolfe is the most iniquitous, for besides being an exploitative bank president he is a cruel landlord and the rigid Calvinist leader of an anti-Catholic organization.

Landlords in Lippard's novels are typically cold-hearted real-estate developers who build huge structures in which they cram as many poor folk as possible in order to turn a quick profit. Israel Bonus of *Memoirs of a Preacher* pays carpenters slave wages to construct the sprawling tenement Bonus Court and then holds "in equal contempt tenants who [can]not pay their rent, and Infidels who [go] about talking of the miseries of the Poor."[9] In *New York* Lippard resurrects Israel Yorke of *The Empire City* to underscore the special cruelty of a banker who becomes a landlord. In one of Yorke's four-story rental buildings many poor families live "like maggots in a stale cheese."[10] Yorke's refusal to allow a starving artist, John Martin, an extension on his rent causes Martin to return to his apartment and light a charcoal and opium fire whose fumes kill him along with his wife and children. When Yorke enters the Martin apartment and discovers his tenants' corpses on the floor, Lippard describes the situation with a typical mixture of grim urban realism and sheer Gothic horror: "Such was the scene which the light disclosed; a scene incredible only to those who, unfamiliar with the ACTUAL of the large city, do not know that all the boasted triumphs of modern civilization but miserably compensate for the POVERTY which it has created, and which stalks side by side with it, like a skeleton beside a painted harlot—a poverty which gives to the phrase, '*I am poor!,*' a despair unknown even in the darkest ages of the most barbarous past" (205).

In some novels Lippard emphasized that politicians were also leagued against the poor. An ardent Democrat who supported such populists as Andrew Jackson while opposing such Whigs as Daniel Webster, Lippard in *The Nazarene* lampooned the Federalist establishment in his portrayal of Mr. Millstone of Milastoga, a presidential nominee surrounded by rich sycophants and representing a party that "scorns [the] People" and "approaches Monarchy."[11] Gabriel Godlike of *The Empire City,* a caricature of Daniel Webster, is a celebrated Washington statesman who uses his oratorical powers to seduce a slave girl, believing that "the most ingenious argument, in law and love, before the Supreme Court, and in the Parlour, commence alike with a—*Lie.*"[12]

In addition to such capitalists and statesmen, Lippard created memorable satirical portraits of newspaper editors, who were usually presented as scandal-mongers making money from the misfortune of others. Although trained as a penny-press reporter and clearly influenced by the style of the new journalism, Lippard sought to distinguish his moral reformism from what he saw as the amoral sensationalism of the penny papers. Whenever Buzby Poodle, editor of the *Daily Black Mail* in *The Quaker City,* needs cash, he simply prints an article charging some prominent Philadelphian with forgery, seduction, or murder, guaranteeing an immediate rise in the paper's circulation and making possible blackmail of the slandered citizen. Similarly, Ishmael Ghoul of *The Empire City* is a "well known editor, who lived upon the vices of the rich and the misfortunes of the poor—who raked palace and hovel, in order to gather food for the morbid appetites of his readers—who, in a word, was the first of that vile breed whose papers, reeking with pollution, and dipped in infamy, seem to have been printed upon one of the 'power presses' of Hell."[13] Lippard's longest parody of the penny press occurs in *Memoirs of a Preacher,* in which he describes the editor Slinkum Scisselby as a "singular phantom of the press, who looked for all the world like the decayed Ghost of some dead paragraph on the state of the money market." Scisselby's *Daily Copper* is "one of those Moral Monsters, which are as necessary to the Great City as malaria to a swamp, or poison to a druggist's shelves"; it is "a kind of infernal organ, doomed to make demoniac discord under ground, and groan in a prolonged anthem, *dollar,* DOLLAR, DOLLAR."[14] It takes all sides to all questions and indifferently libels and praises everybody in turn.

In the course of his literary career Lippard satirized, along with the above figures, factory owners, slave-hunters, land sharks, monopolists, and lawyers. His stinging caricatures, enlivened by urban Gothic imagery, were at once entertaining and trenchant, winning for him both notoriety and respect as a crusader against social wrongdoing.

As his fiction became popular with the masses, Lippard increasingly complemented his attacks on the elite with sympathetic portraits of the poor and with socialist argument. In some respects, his career paralleled that of Eugene Sue. Formerly a maritime adventure novelist, Sue began *The Mysteries of Paris* primarily as another exercise in sensationalism, viewing the raw argot and colorful criminals of the Parisian underground as a new and exciting premise for a salable book. It was only after the first twelve segments of the novel were immensely popular with poor people throughout France that Sue began to infuse socialist commentary into his novel. The class of whom Sue wrote became the class for whom he wrote, making his democratic socialism chiefly the outgrowth of the political demands of his readers.[15]

Lippard began his career writing penny-press exposés, Gothic narratives, and adventurous Revolutionary War stories. Only after the first several segments of *The Quaker City* were avidly read by the masses—and often criticized or ignored by the elite—did he admit poor characters and low-life scenes into his fiction with any frequency. It is notable that the confrontation between the poor John Davis and the banker Job Joneson, as well as a scene of fifty vagabonds and criminals called "the outcasts of the Quaker City," occur toward the end of the novel, suggesting that Lippard was trying to cater politically to the lowbrow audience he had gained through his chiefly sensational early segments.

Lippard's increasingly political self-image was reflected in his shifting views about the function of fiction. In 1842, as Billy Brier in *The Spirit of the Times,* he voiced an early interest in sheer escapism by having Brier whimsically dream of becoming a novelist who would "daub the brush thick" with romance and action, "so thick that the paint couldn't be laid on any thicker."[16] Seven years later a much more socially minded Lippard would write that "a literature which does not work practically, for the advancement of social reform, or which is too good or too dignified to picture the wrongs of the great mass of humanity, is just good for nothing at all."[17] Lippard had become what Joseph Jackson calls a "poet of the proletariat" in part because the proletariat was buying his fiction.[18]

Although analogous to Sue in his increasingly strong political identification with his readers, from the beginning Lippard was more egalitarian than the rather paternalistic Sue. Sue was an atheistic dandy who had vests of every color of the rainbow, always wore gloves (never the same pair twice), changed his clothes three times a day, and ate only at the most fashionable restaurants. Theoretically a democrat, he was secretly horrified by the riffraff of the Parisian streets. To do research for *The Mysteries of Paris* he put on poor men's clothing and toured Parisian saloons and brothels, accompanied by a muscular friend who served as a bodyguard.[19] This paternalism was reflected in Sue's characterization of Rudolph, the wealthy protagonist of *The Mysteries of Paris* who disguises himself as a poor man and descends

into the Parisian underworld, always protecting and rewarding
the virtuous poor while punishing the wicked like an angel from
above.

Lippard, in contrast, was educated in poverty, social upheaval,
and misfortune long before he began writing fiction. From the
painful perspective of a youth virtually abandoned by his parents
and then disinherited, he witnessed the dockworkers' and weavers'
strikes, economic crashes, bank closures, and racial and religious
riots of Philadelphia's turbulent Jacksonian period. Although in
the mid-1840s he also began to strike a dandified pose by wearing
velvet vests and dramatic capes, his populist sympathies were
strong from his early childhood onward. His humanitarianism
was apparent even in his primarily sensational early writings:
witness the poor men's revolts against tyranny in "Philippe de
Agramont" and *The Ladye Annabel,* or his praise of common
soldiers of the American Revolution in *The Citizen Soldier,* or his
editorials against the Girard College debacle and the Nicholas
Biddle affair. The popularity of *The Quaker City* was merely the
catalyst for fuller expression of humanitarian and socialist leanings
that had always been latent.

Once Lippard began portraying the poor at length—in the
final installments of *The Quaker City,* in *The Nazarene,* and in
most of his later city novels—he did so without Sue's paternalism.
The "consolatory structure" of *The Mysteries of Paris,* by which
a rich man is always on hand to save or punish the poor,[20] is
largely absent from Lippard's novels. Lippard's wealthy characters
are ordinarily unregenerate figures who cheat the poor instead of
aiding them, while the weavers, seamstresses, and factory workers
they victimize often resort to crime or suicide not because of
inherent sinfulness but because of exploitation from above. Lippard viewed poverty as a social ill produced by economic inequities
rather than as a personal one growing from idleness or irreligion.
He saw through the hopeful Horatio Alger myth of rags-to-riches
success even before it became popular, and long before the Social
Gospel novelists of the 1890s he directly attacked the common
American outlook that "any one who does right can get along.

It's only the idle, the improvident, or the criminal, who are poor."[21]

While sympathetic toward the urban poor, Lippard did not go to the opposite extreme of idealizing them or meliorating their plight; he avoided a common tendency among such sentimental-domestic novelists as Fanny Fern, Susan Warner, and Maria Cummins to present indigent but cheerfully pious protagonists who bravely endure setbacks with the knowledge that their virtue will be rewarded in the end. Lippard concentrated on what he called "the dread realities of poverty."[22] In *The Nazarene,* capturing the "utter misery and degradation" of a tenement district in Philadelphia, he describes how human "shapes of misery wound along the dark alley, mingling together, until looking along the prospect of wretchedness you beheld nothing but a far spreading vista of rags and sores, blindness and misery, lameness, disease, starvation and crime."[23] Elsewhere in *The Nazarene* he takes us into a weaver's home, filled with disease and blasted dreams, and into a factory, "a Slave-House" that is "crowded by miserable forms, swarming to their labor in rooms rendered loathsome by foul air, and filled with floating particles of cotton, that seize upon the lungs and bite them into rottenness" (166). Lippard intensified his depiction of the wretchedness of factory work in "The Sisterhood of the Green Veil" (1849) and especially in *Adonai: The Pilgrim of Eternity,* in which a factory owner tells the pilgrims how " 'we who adore Capital, celebrate his worship by chaining [men, women, and children] to the wheels of iron machinery. The wheel whirls, and first the soul, then the body . . . is crushed.' "[24] In "The Dark Sabbath" (1849), "Jesus and the Poor" (1849), and *'Bel of Prairie Eden* Lippard laments banks' mishandling of the legacy of Stephen Girard by describing waifs sinking into poverty and crime because of long delays in the construction of Girard's college for orphans. In *New York* a seamstress, paid a mere pittance for clothes she has toiled over for long hours, returns to her hovel where her father is dying and where she recognizes that her only alternatives are suicide or prostitution.

The kinds of grim low-life vignettes Lippard created would be transformed by such later novelists as Émile Zola, Frank Norris,

and Theodore Dreiser into entire novels. While Lippard avoided
the simplistic optimism and implied or overt elitism of many of
his literary contemporaries, he also managed to fabricate some
poor protagonists manifesting verve, healthy rebelliousness, and
concrete political knowledge. Early in his career his most independent characters were brave Continental soldiers and brash
Leatherstocking figures fighting Tory aristocrats during the Revolution. In *The Quaker City* he briefly summoned a veteran of the
Revolution into Philadelphia to indict foreign missionaries who
ignore the poor at home.

In his later city novels his poor heroes become more fully
developed, as well as more militant and political. John Hoffman
of *The Empire City,* a crusty mechanic and ex-convict possessing
"a dauntless will, a ferocious energy," is a crudely sketched vernacular hero with a sardonic wit that presages Mark Twain's
fictional personae and some of Harriet Beecher Stowe's lowly
characters.[25] A herculean spokesman for the masses who avenges
capitalist exploitation by killing the wealthy villain of the novel,
Hoffman is an agent for Lippard's satire on elite corruption and
especially for the exposure of the cruelties of the American prison
system. In *New York* Lippard brought to American fiction its
first extensively described socialist hero in the person of Arthur
Dermoyne, a tough shoemaker who impugns businessmen and
hypocritical preachers and at the end leads a band of three hundred
laborers to the western frontier to form a communistic community. In both *The Empire City* and *New York* Lippard's increased
militancy is evidenced by three separate scenes involving poor
tenants or escaped slaves who in secret "courts of ten millions"
bring to trial landlords, moguls, or slave-hunters whom they
strongly denounce and savagely punish.

While creating the period's most comprehensive fictional in-
dictments of the rich and defenses of the poor, Lippard also
commented on slavery, the problems of Native Americans,
women's rights, land reform, European socialist theory, and
industrialism.

Lippard's attitude toward slavery was complex; one commen-
tator's claim that Lippard was a famous abolitionist who was the

first to turn Abraham Lincoln against slavery is a pure fabrication.[26] Though painfully conscious of the southern Negro's plight, Lippard was more concerned with the white slavery in northern factories than with black slavery on southern plantations. He feared that a civil war might shatter the holy Union established by America's Founding Fathers, and some of the villains of his late novels are slave-hunters and abolitionists whose intrusive crossing of sectional lines and whose inflammatory rhetoric Lippard feared as potential destroyers of that Union. Also, Lippard had a habit, common enough among novelists and journalists of his day but seemingly incompatible with his egalitarianism, of describing Negroes as comically obsequious, brutish, stupid, and volatile. This was especially true in his early novels. In *Herbert Tracy* he says that the protagonist's fawning black servant, Charles de Fust, had a "general figure as grotesque in outline, and as ludicrous in proportion, as though Nature had turned caricaturist, and manufactured a walking libel upon the whole monkey tribe."[27] In *The Quaker City* Lippard adopts a similarly racist attitude toward Mary Arlington's servant Lewey (who calls Mary an angel while admitting that as a black man he will probably be barred from heaven), toward Devil-Bug's Negro helpers Musquito and Glow-worm, and toward Fitz-Cowles's lackey Endymion. Even in Lippard's later novels the most sympathetically portrayed black characters are "white Negroes," usually escaped slaves whose light skin and blue eyes attest to the fact that white plantation owners are among their sires.

Nevertheless, Lippard remains one of the first Americans who protested against slavery in fiction and who fashioned heroic black characters. Despite his caricatures of blacks in *The Quaker City*, he included in Devil-Bug's dream of Philadelphia in 1850 a scene of "the slaves of the city, white and black, . . . the slaves of the cotton Lord and the factory Prince" manacled and lashed by cruel businessmen.[28] Black Sampson, the muscular Negro member of the Oath-Bound Five in Lippard's Brandywine legend, avenges the murder of his mistress by valiantly marching into battle with his murderous dog "Debbil," who delights in ripping open the throats of Tories. In the second part of *The Empire City* Lippard

penned America's first fictional indictment of the Fugitive Slave
Law, the law that more than any other caused the split between
the North and the South. Lippard again protested against the law
in "Eleanor; or, Slave Catching in the Quaker City," and in *New
York* he showed a "Black Senate" of escaped slaves beating to
death a mercenary slave-hunter. Although Lippard never reached
the ardent abolitionism of Harriet Beecher Stowe, he can be
credited with preceding and in some ways surpassing Stowe in
the fictional portrayal of the divisiveness and violence caused by
slavery.

Lippard was aware of the miseries of another ethnic subgroup
in America, the Indians on the western frontier. Lamenting the
collapse of Native American culture in the face of encroaching
white civilization, he noted that Indians, who were here long
before whites, were being cheated by land buyers and corrupted
by pioneers. In *The Nazarene* he writes: "From the day that the
Pilgrim Fathers began to murder them for their land, as wild
beasts are slain for their skin, down until the present year of our
Lord, 1846, one bloody catalogue of wrong has been the Index
to the history of the Indian race."[29] He illustrates this point
through a plot in *The Nazarene* involving a tribe of Indians whose
lands on the Mississippi are bought at unfairly low prices by
eastern bankers, and whose people are decimated by the venereal
disease and alcohol brought West by white explorers. To oppose
such injustice he has a noble chieftain's son, Yonawaga, travel
to Washington, D.C., to lobby for legislation that would save
"the last wreck of a mighty people" (108). Likewise, Lippard
begins *'Bel of Prairie Eden* by picturing a lone Indian weeping
over the forced westward movement of his race. In *The Rose of
Wissahikon* Lippard underscores the courage and patriotism of
Indians by having the warrior Wayaniko save a woman from
seducers and then deliver a copy of the Declaration of Independence to American troops in an exhausting hundred-mile ride.

Women's rights was another current issue that drew Lippard's
attention. Arguing in *The Man with the Mask* that only women
should serve as midwives, he stressed women's intellectual ca-
pabilities: "Women can be educated, and well educated in the

most difficult branches of the Medical profession."[30] In 1850 he wrote a glowing review of the feminist Lucretia Mott's "Discourse on Woman," which he found "well worthy to be in the hands of every female in the land who feels an interest in this question of the social elevation of her sex."[31] In the same year he helped organize a union for Philadelphia seamstresses on the belief that woman's lot was worse than that of men and even of slaves, and that only through organization would woman successfully advance her cause. Lippard conceived the idea of a women's branch of the Brotherhood of the Union; not only was the Home Communion formed in 1867, but by 1980 it had become the most active segment of the order.

We need not turn to Lippard's reformist late years, however, to find evidence of his interest in feminism. While many popular novelists of his period were writing fiction filled with cherubic girls or sentimentally pious women, Lippard often created heroines who were independent, frankly sexual, or interestingly depraved. Dora Livingstone stands out as an especially intriguing figure, but other females in *The Quaker City*—Mabel, Mary, Long-haired Bess, Mother Nancy Perkins—also display a complex range of passions and allegiances unseen in most fictional heroines of the day. In his Revolutionary legends Lippard shows several "Hero-Women" joining men in battle, and in the midst of one legend he pauses to make a semantic distinction popular with many feminists today: "The woman—I use that word, for to me it expresses all that is pure in passion, or holy in humanity, while your word—lady—means nothing but ribbons and millinery."[32] In *Blanche of Brandywine* Lady Isidore, who like several Lippard heroines dresses in men's clothing, overcomes men in sword fights, while Blanche Walford spiritedly resists lecherous pursuers. The poor women of Lippard's urban fiction, though buffeted by poverty and tempted by prostitution, usually remain unruffled, as suggested by Lippard's description of a seamstress who in the face of misfortune "did not start, and call down thunders, and burst into those torrents of epithets and adjectives with which some lady-novelists make lurid their pages; for she was not the kind of woman you find in some specimens of lady-

literature, but a real woman! much tried, deeply suffering—
maybe, somewhat fallen—but still a woman and not a tornado
in petticoats."[33]

In addition to portraying women who were frequently independent or richly passionate, Lippard coupled pleas for social
reform with a unique amalgamation of foreign socialist theory
and historical interpretation of class struggles. Although Karl
Marx's *Communist Manifesto* was published in London in 1848,
it did not appear in America until after Lippard's death, and there
is no evidence that Lippard knew Marx's work. Instead, in the
late 1840s Lippard began to fuse his own political theories with
those of several European and American labor reformers. Although he showed only passing interest in the Fourierist com-
munities formed in the United States in the 1840s, he thought
that Charles Fourier had *"discovered* the true Law which God has
given for the government of the social world," a law that *"har-
monizes* Capital and Labor, and invests Industry with . . . attraction and variety."[34] He had high praise for the French socialist
Louis Blanc,who believed that all crime was due to poverty and
that the state must eliminate competition. He warmly supported
the communists and subversive societies that helped precipitate
the European revolutions of 1848. He even dared to defend an
earlier French revolutionary, Robespierre, in a day when most
Americans vilified Robespierre as a godless incendiary. Surveying
American history, Lippard found precedent for communism and
land reform in the eighteenth-century pietist community at
Ephrata. Among nineteenth-century reform currents, he was most
influenced by the agrarian and cooperative movements. Following
the lead of the land reformer George Henry Evans, he called for
the free distribution of Western homesteads to America's urban
poor. An ardent supporter of the rising cooperative movement
of the 1850s, he hoped that each circle of his Brotherhood would
become a "Union of Capital" in order to cut out the money-
making middlemen who, he believed, prevented workers from
enjoying the full fruits of their labor. Onto these ideas Lippard
grafted medieval ritualism, nonsectarian Christianity, and Ma-
sonic fraternalism to produce a highly eclectic social outlook.

Among the first Americans to be branded as "a Red," Lippard in 1849 retaliated against conservative critics by writing a humorous story about a country bumpkin, Gregory Grunakle, who reads in the newspapers terrifying stories about a three-headed monster—"Socialist, Red Republican, and Fourierite"—who is desolating New York City. Packing up his pistols with the aim of killing the monster, Grunakle spends a week in New York confronting the worst people he can find—a slanderous editor, a venal merchant, complacent Trinity Church members, a lecherous rich man, a moral editor who has abandoned a woman—only to discover that none of them is the monster he seeks and that in fact each vehemently denounces the three-headed beast.[35]

In *Adonai: The Pilgrim of Eternity* Lippard replaced the defensive sarcasm of the Grunakle sketch with a thoroughgoing, quite serious presentation of his social views. The most original feature of the novel, beside its stylistic mixture of allegory and realism, is its historical interpretation of progressive thought. According to the Scientific Socialism of Marx and Engels, such Utopian Socialists as Saint-Simon and Fourier had failed to recognize socialism as a necessary outgrowth of historical class struggles between freeman and slave, patrician and plebeian, baron and serf, and so forth. Without having read Marx, Lippard in *Adonai* approximated some of Marx's ideas by presenting a Christian in early Roman times, imprisoned by Nero for his heretical beliefs, traveling forward through the centuries to witness successive conflicts between oppressors and oppressed—between tyrannical medieval Popes and the gulled masses, the sixteenth-century Catholic church and Martin Luther, Great Britain and the thirteen colonies, nineteenth-century European monarchists and French socialists, American capitalists and poor factory workers, land sharks and homestead settlers. To be sure, Lippard's view of history was not precisely that of Marx. While Marx was a disciplined social scientist who carefully traced economic conflicts that he believed would eventually give birth to a healthy socialist society, Lippard was an impressionistic, imaginative historian whose vision of the past was colored by religious mysticism and ardent partiotism. The fact remains, however, that Lippard to some degree possessed the historical consciousness that Marx prized and that most American labor spokesmen lacked. Also, when Lippard turned from the past to visions of the future, he had the foresight to draw an ambiguous picture of industrialized America: "All over the land the roar of the steam engine was heard. The clang of iron wheels upon the roads of iron, broke harshly through the stillness. The lighted windows of the Factory blazed through the darkness on every hand. From Golden California to the Empire City, huge cities reared their heads, swarming with countless souls. An empire no less bewildering in the suddenness of its growth than in the god-like glory—or yet awful gloom—of its Future."[36]

Legendary History: The Interplay of Fact and Fiction

Adonai was essentially a combination of the egalitarian social commentary of Lippard's urban fiction and the creative historicism of his patriotic legends. While Lippard's city novels might appear more interesting to modern readers than his legendary histories, it is the latter that have had the more lasting impact upon American culture. The millions of Americans today who believe that on July 4, 1776, the Liberty Bell was rung to proclaim freedom throughout the land, after fifty-six Founding Fathers had communally signed the Declaration of Independence, are indebted to Lippard, who created the myth in one of his Revolutionary legends for the *Saturday Courier*.

The facts of the signing of the Declaration of Independence are not nearly as dramatic as Lippard led many Americans to believe. In reality, the Declaration was adopted on July 2, 1776. The preamble was adopted on July 4, but the signing did not begin until August 2, and the list of signers as it now stands was not completed until January 18, 1777. The congressional proceedings were quiet and private, and there was no public celebration the day the preamble was adopted. The Declaration was proclaimed and read in public by the Sheriff of the City and County at noon July 8, 1776, in the State House Square, and reportedly there were bonfires and a general ringing of bells.

In Lippard's version, on July 4 an old man climbs to the State House bell tower, telling a little blue-eyed boy below to yell "Ring!" as soon as he hears from the recently convened Continental Congress that the Declaration has been signed. After a long description of the fifty-six signers inside Independence Hall hearing a patriotic speech by an unnamed orator, Lippard has John Hancock emerge to speak with the boy, who runs to the State House with the glorious message of Liberty. The Liberty Bell tolls triumphantly and there is a mass celebration. The perpetuation of Lippard's myth resulted not only from its powerful jingoistic appeal but also from its being accepted as fact by some important historians. In *The Pictorial Field Book of the Revolution* (1850) Benson J. Lossing stated plainly what Lippard had described floridly, retaining all of Lippard's incidents and characters. The story was later repeated in John Franklin Jameson's famous *Dictionary of United States History* (1894) and, most remarkable of all, in John H. Hazelton's exhaustively documented *The Declaration of Independence* (1906). Although more recent scholars have confirmed Hazelton's passing remark that the story might be apocryphal, the Liberty Bell has become a sacred relic venerated by thousands of visitors to Philadelphia and widely exploited by politicians and advertising people—all as a direct result of George Lippard's sky-scraping fancy.[37]

Lippard's development of the Liberty Bell legend illustrates the poetic license Lippard felt free to take with history. The fabricated story of the old man, the boy, the communal signing, and the ringing of the bell was contained in the first version of the legend in the *Courier* on January 3, 1846, and it remained throughout three subsequent versions in the *Courier*, in *The Rose of Wissahikon*, and in *Washington and His Generals*. Lippard's biggest problem concerned the identity of the orator in Independence Hall. In the 1846 *Courier* version Lippard called the speaker Patrick Henry, but the obvious fallacy of this detail impelled him to change the name to John Witherspoon. Trying to cover up Lippard's mistake, the *Courier* explained the revised second version as follows: "Between the person who copied the author's ms. and the proofreader an error crept in, the substitution of the name Patrick Henry for John Witherspoon. Henry, as everyone knows, was not among the signers."[38] But Witherspoon was another wrong guess, and in the final version of the legend Lippard simply referred to "the Unknown Orator."

Lippard's tampering with historical fact did not escape the notice of some of his contemporary critics. The *Saturday Evening Post* complained that Lippard had "taken the liberty to palter with and corrupt the pages of history," while A. J. H. Duganne commented that "it requires a caoutchouc conscience to tolerate the aberrations of Mr. L's historic muse, a lady of most uncommon looseness of character, who takes unbecoming liberties with the dead and living, coquetting with Fact in a way that shocks our notions of literary propriety."[39] Thompson Westcott, noting several discrepancies between the facts of the signing of the Declaration and Lippard's Liberty Bell legend, sarcastically said that for Lippard fact was just "another melancholy proof of the stupidity of History!"[40]

Such carping did not deter Lippard, who believed he was performing an inestimable service to his country by adding color, warmth, and patriotic emphasis to dry history. "It must be confessed," he wrote in *Legends of Mexico,* "that the thing which generally passes for History, is the most impudent, swaggering bully, the most graceless braggart, the most reckless equivocator that ever staggered forth on the great stage of the world."[41] He voiced his priorities by defining a legend as "one of those heartwarm stories, which, quivering in rude, earnest language from the lips of a spectator of a battle, or the survivor of some event of olden time, fill up the cold outlines of history, and clothe the skeleton with flesh and blood, give it eyes and tongue, force it at once to look into our eyes and talk with us!" (55–56).

Lippard's fictional embellishment of history had precedent in the novels of Walter Scott and G. P. R. James, the poetry of the French reformer Michelet, and the historical fiction of such American authors as James Fenimore Cooper, Catherine Sedgwick, Lydia Maria Child, John Neal, and William Gilmore Simms. In such works as *Herbert Tracy, The Rose of Wissahikon,* and *Paul Ardenheim* Lippard followed the example of these authors by concentrating on romantic intrigue or conflict among fictional characters who remained on the fringes of famous historical occurrences. In his legends about the Germantown and Brandywine battles, as well as in *Washington and His Generals, Legends of Mexico,* and *Washington and His Men,* he took the more original step of highlighting fictionalized versions of the historical events themselves, such as Washington or Taylor rallying their men and leading them into battle.

In both types of fiction, but especially in the latter, Lippard was chiefly interested in recreating history in such a way as to accentuate the courage, magnanimity, piety, and democratic sympathies of bygone or current heroes. If Lippard was most radical in his urban novels, he was most reactionary in his historical legends. Appalled by the corruption he saw in modern cities, in his historical fiction he revisited times when, he thought, life was simpler and issues were more clearly defined: the time of Christ, when the faith of the Carpenter of Nazareth was not yet twisted by thousands of jarring sects; the fifteenth century, when the secret Brotherhood of the Rosy Cross performed its ritualistic ceremonies;[42] the early eighteenth century, when German pietists in Pennsylvania observed a creedless, mystical faith in the sylvan peace of the Wissahickon valley; the time of the American Revolution, before divisive factions and commercial exploitation had threatened to destroy the American Union. Most of Lippard's legends about the American past were embellishments of incidents selected from John Fanning Watson's *Annals of Philadelphia* (1823; expanded 1844) and Jared Sparks's *The Life of George Washington* (1839). Lippard fleshed out factual information from such histories with fanciful oral traditions derived from local folklore or interviews with Revolutionary War veterans, with stories from eighteenth-century newspapers, and often with tales spun by his own imagination. One of his main goals was to retrieve Pennsylvania's settlers, battles, and military heroes from the obscurity to which New England historians had generally consigned them.

To say that Lippard was nostalgic for the past is not to say that he whitewashed it; quite to the contrary, more acutely than most historical novelists of his day, he recognized the cruelty and violence that inevitably darkened pious dreams and heroic deeds. Moreover, he was ahead of his time in complementing his veneration of Revolutionary heroes with balanced appraisals of such reputed villains as Thomas Paine and Benedict Arnold. Unlike most historians and readers of the period, who were wont to dismiss Paine as an infidel, Lippard helped to restore Paine's reputation by pointing to the bold democratic sentiments of *Common Sense,* which he believed were more crucial to an understanding of Paine than the deism of *The Age of Reason.* His legends and lectures about Paine "aroused a great deal of attention," causing "an increased sale of Paine's works" and impelling a late-nineteenth-century historian to praise Lippard for bravely defending Paine when such defense meant ostracism.[43] As for Arnold, Lippard reasonably noted that one should not forget the general's military heroism early in the war, as well as the machinations of his wife and Philadelphia politicians that helped precipitate his treason.

Although Lippard never succinctly summarized his view of history in chronological order, such a summary may be gleaned from various legends. In his eyes, the most peaceful moment in the past nineteen centuries was Christ's early childhood. Christ's adolescence and adulthood established a pattern of innocence, strength, and sympathy for the poor opposed by malice, duplicity, and elitism that was reenacted throughout the centuries. Christian history was a sequence of bloody persecution waged by such figures as the inquisitors, John Calvin, King George III, and modern aristocrats against the poor, who found successive champions in leaders of medieval brotherhoods, William Penn, the Revolutionary heroes, Andrew Jackson, Zachary Taylor, and the French socialists. The rigidity, theological exactitude, and viciousness of the persecutors contrasted sharply with the warmth, simplicity, and sturdiness of the persecuted. Lippard saw America as the Last Altar of Human Brotherhood that has seen three great epochs: the Epoch of the Apostles, in which William Penn and other tolerant Pennsylvania settlers reared the altar of Brotherhood in the New World; the Epoch of the Deliverer, when George

Washington and his followers scourged America's oppressors and freed her poor; and the ongoing Epoch of the Crowned Avenger, a time of tremendous battles between oppressors and oppressed that is preparing for the Universal Liberator who will arrive sometime in the late nineteenth century. Lippard viewed his own Brotherhood of the Union as the nation's chief sustainer of the medieval rituals, Revolutionary ideals, and militant anticapitalism that would speed the coming of the Universal Liberator.

Lippard's periodic changes in emphasis, growing cynicism, and recognition of irrational drives made his political attitudes more complex than this summary suggests. Even if his view of history had been unchanging and unalloyed, however, it would be interesting enough, for it shows an active mind grappling with past events and current problems in an effort to make combinations that had never been expressed before.

Some of Lippard's most popular legends were those in which he yoked together Biblical and Revolutionary scenes. As a Revolutionary historian he looked upon himself as "a Pilgrim in holy ground" encountering "the Heroes of the Revolution—the Man-Gods of our Past."[44] Accordingly, he created several scenes that interpreted Washington's mission in biblical terms: in *Paul Ardenheim* a Wissahickon alchemist consecrates Washington as the Deliverer prophesied in Revelations; in the Brandywine legend Christ's temptation in the desert is paralleled by a scene in which the British general William Howe tries to bribe Washington into treason by offering him a dukedom; when Washington prays for victory while kneeling between British and American lines, Lippard compares him to "JESUS, with the blood-drops starting from cheek and brow" as he "plead for the salvation of the world."[45] Lippard imbued other scenes and characters with religious significance. In one legend he has a preacher several decades before the Revolution have a vision of a bloody massacre in the Quaker Meeting House at Brandywine, a vision that horribly proves accurate. Such apocalyptic supernatural prophecy appears in the Tory Lord Percy of Monthermer's dream of his grisly death in battle, as well as in Blanche Walford's vision of two spirit-hosts waging war in the heavens. In Lippard's religious imagination, Benedict Arnold after his treason was like Lucifer after the fall, while Thomas Paine was recovered from infidelity by his alleged deathbed conversion to Christianity.

The Revolutionary ground Lippard revisited was holy but also was drenched in blood and tears. At the same time that he deified Washington, he wished to humanize him, just as in his biblical legends he wished to humanize Christ. Attacking the usual representation of Washington as a "figure of mist and frost-work," Lippard tried to portray "the living, throbbing, flesh and blood" of "WASHINGTON THE MAN."[46] As in his city fiction he often shifted between Gothic supernaturalism and urban realism, so in his historical fiction he balanced mythical heightening of the past with verisimilitude. Thus, his legends are peopled not only with glorious generals or fantastic alchemists and astrologers but also with unsung poor soldiers, such as a mechanic who avenges the murder of his wife by fighting Tories to the death, or the Oath-Bound Five at Brandywine, or the hunters and farmers who battle bravely at Germantown. As mentioned in Chapter 2, Lippard periodically permitted his patriotic respect for Revolutionary heroes to dissolve into a realistic recognition of the viciousness and horror of war. In *Washington and His Generals,* after describing the charred corpse of a Quaker who was murdered by the British, Lippard writes: "War has been painted too long as a pretty thing, spangled with buttons, fluttering with ribbons, waving with plumes. Let us learn to look upon it as it is; a horrible bandit, reeking with the blood of the innocent, the knife of murder in his hand, the fire of carnage in his eye" (359). In *Legends of Mexico* Lippard illustrates "the reeking Golgothas of War" with such details as a soldier "torn in two by a combination of horrible missiles, which bear his mangled flesh away, whirling a bloody shower through the air. That thing beneath the horse's feet, with the head bent back, until it touches the heels, that mass of bloody flesh, in which the face, feet and brains alone are distinguishable, was only a moment past a living man."[47]

The vividness and energy of such descriptions combined with Lippard's religious and patriotic mythicism to make his historical legends not only extremely popular but also widely imitated and even plagiarized. The appearance between 1845 and 1848 of several volumes of historical legends by authors hoping to capitalize on Lippard's success induced Lippard to preface an explanation of his theory of legends with the wry remark: "So many gentlemen have done me the kindness to write 'Legends' since I began it, and in certain cases, to borrow mine, without so much as a bow for common courtesy, that I am forced to define my position."[48] If Lippard had deep contempt for the "Rancheros of literature" who copied him and for "Critics, Reviewers, and all other Pigmies of the pen" who lambasted him,[49] he could boast of many American readers who admired his legends. He concluded *Washington and His Generals* by quoting passages from a letter sent him by one of Zachary Taylor's soldiers at Monterey. The soldier describes how at night he and his weary comrades often gathered around the campfire while someone read aloud one of Lippard's Revolutionary legends from the *Courier*. "Believe me, Sir," the soldier writes, "those things made our hearts feel warm—they nerved our arm for the battle! When we read of the old times of our Flag, we swore in our hearts, never to disgrace it!"[50]

It is difficult to measure precisely the impact that Lippard's legends had upon the American popular imagination. A conservative assessment is that Lippard was the most visible of several novelists of the period who brought to historical fiction a new fiery jingoism that kindled the chauvinistic pride of thousands of Americans. A bolder, yet not unwarranted, generalization is that Lippard shaped this nation's patriotic self-image to a degree equalled by no American novelist before him and by few novelists of any period.

The far-reaching significance of the Liberty Bell myth alone supports this generalization, but in fact this was just one of several legends to survive his death. Washington's being offered a dukedom by General Howe and his kneeling to pray between opposing lines at Brandywine are fictions that were accepted by many school children and adults throughout the nineteenth century and into the early decades of the twentieth. As recently as 1919 historians were still digging up turf in the Brandywine area searching for the remains of Lord Percy of Monthermer, unaware that Percy was merely a creation of Lippard's fancy. Lippard's legend of the dying Benedict Arnold donning his old Continental war jacket in a final moment of resurgent patriotism remained in 1917 "a very effective and popular" story in American grade schools.[51] And in 1939 a Philadelphia newspaper could note that *Paul Ardenheim* was chiefly responsible for reviving several myths about early German pietists in the Wissahickon area, myths that "have been flourishing gayly ever since."[52] The persistence of such legends suggests that Lippard succeeded not only in embellishing history but also in helping to create it.

Chapter Four

The Gleam on the Sword: Lippard and Religion

John Bell Bouton pronounced religion "the leading trait in [Lippard's] character" and noted "the soft, sweet aspirations that run through his most terrible books, like the delicate filigree of gold upon a warrior's sword."[1] Dismayed by the hypocrisy and theological divisiveness of contemporary religionists, Lippard sought to replace conventional Christianity with a humanistic religion that combined warm sentiment and militant socialism. Like many American writers of his day, he used fiction to detach religion from theology and place it in a new secular context. Unlike most, he reached affirmation only after assaulting the reader's sensibilities with scathing satire and portraits of terror and perversity. His search for alternatives to theology and corrupt religion led him into periodic infatuations with such pseudosciences as astrology, animal magnetism, and spiritualism. Beneath his rather frenetic experimentation with various faiths and fads lurked the gloomy suspicion that moral certainty was a chimera and that man's only hope was to grasp the behavioral, political essentials of a secularized Christianity.

Religious Satire and Affirmation

Lippard's satire on contemporary religion and his reconstruction of faith outside of creed both had precedent in earlier American fiction. Such works as Philip Freneau's *Letters on Various Subjects* (1799) and the anonymously written *The Yankee Traveller* (1817), *The Life and Adventures of Obadiah Benjamin Franklin Bloomfield* (1818), *Confessions of a Magdalene* (1831), and *The Hyp-*

ocrite (1844) exposed the squabbling polemicism and secret licentiousness of Protestant clergymen. Such nativist works as George Bourne's *Lorette* (1833), Rebecca Reed's *Six Months in a Convent* (1835), and Maria Monk's *Awful Disclosures of . . . the Hotel Dieu Nunnery at Montreal* (1836) directed the charge of ministerial corruption against Roman Catholic priests. Lippard exaggerated the salaciousness of both anti-Protestant and nativist satire while leaving behind the anti-Catholicism of the latter. On the affirmative side, Lippard multiplied antitheological devices that had been increasingly used by American fictionists since the late eighteenth century, devices that included portraits of the human Jesus, familiar views of an earthlike heaven, and representations of heroic, emotional religious duty in common life.[2] Whereas the typical American religious novelist assumed either a combative or an inspirational stance, Lippard brought together vicious condemnation and benign affirmation, suggesting that the gleam of religious consolation could be enjoyed only after the sword of satire had done its reformist work.

Lippard's main religious point was that the creedless and egalitarian religion of the Carpenter of Nazareth had over the course of centuries been spoiled by persecution, theological warfare, and elitist complacency. In Lippard's eyes, the medieval Catholic church had buried Jesus' simple religion under ceremonial rites and gilded pomp. Lippard saw Protestantism as a bold and necessary step toward religious purification, but he thought that major flaws in the original conception of Protestantism had led to its current fallen condition. Martin Luther, he wrote, was "a noble man of genius, who had not the courage to go the whole way,—to declare the right of every man to Land and Home in this world, as well as to Hope in the next." By freeing man spiritually but not temporally or economically, Luther's views culminated "in this Nineteenth Century, in a race of teachers, who do not worship a Pope, or bow down to a silver image of Christ, but who do worship a Banker and bow to the silver image of a Dollar," making Protestantism "the paid vassal of usurped Capital."[3] Sensuality, another vice Lippard found common among contemporary clergymen, was prefigured in the "gross and beastly" Protestantism of Henry VIII, in imitation of whom the Church of England for three centuries "aped the vices, without imitating the virtues of the Romish Church" (133).

Worst of all was the coldly logical, grimly deterministic Protestantism of John Calvin, who preached a religion *"without a heart,"* one "that *reasons* but cannot *feel"* (133). No pagan mythologist, Lippard wrote, had ever created a being "so dark, so unpitying, so remorseless" as Calvin's God, no blasphemer had ever "so befouled . . . the human soul" as had Calvin "by his cold-blooded Logic" (134). Calvin's torturing of the heretic Michael Servetus, Lippard argued, set an example of persecution and hatred that was followed by rigid New England Puritans and by nineteenth-century nativists. Also, the Calvinist distinction between the elect and the damned found secular enactment in contemporary class conflicts between the rich and the poor, making "the Modern Oligarchy of the Money Power . . . the richest blossom of John Calvin's idea" (134).

Lippard was disappointed not only in historical Protestantism but also in several of its descendants in nineteenth-century America. By the time he began writing fiction, heated doctrinal controversies between orthodox Trinitarians and liberal Unitarians had been raging for years in New England, while in the 1830s the nativist protest against the arrival of growing numbers of Irish and European emigrants brought to a boil the anti-Catholicism that gave rise to the powerful Know-Nothing party. Highly emotional revivals sparked the dramatic expansion of the Methodist and Baptist denominations, and in the 1840s William Miller set several successive dates for the apocalyptic end of the world prophesied in Revelations. Surveying this stormy religious scene, Lippard wrote: "[W]hat Orthodoxies and Heterodoxies battle with each other; what sterile opinions gripe each other by the throat! All is strife, unrest, and clamor!" (137).

Lippard was especially alarmed by the great Native American riots of 1844, in which groups of enraged Protestants went on two murderous rampages through poor Irish districts in Philadelphia. Unlike such popular novelists as Ned Buntline and A. J. H. Duganne, who became active in the Know-Nothing party,

Lippard often attacked the persecuting temper of anti-Catholic nativists and the smear tactics of their fiction. Moreover, he frequently praised the aesthetic rituals of Catholicism and the heroism of Catholic soldiers during the American Revolution. On the other hand, he had a deep antipathy toward such zealous Roman Catholics as John Joseph Hughes, the New York prelate who wanted to take the Protestant Bible out of public school classrooms, and Orestes Brownson, the exponent of intellectual Catholicism. Lippard's two-sided attitude toward the Catholic question was reflected in the differences between *The Nazarene,* in which he caricatured nativists, and *New York,* in which he exposed Roman Catholics who wished to infiltrate American schools and government.

Lippard opposed theological rigidity and cruel persecution on the part of any denomination, Protestant or Catholic, just as he lamented actual instances of ministerial depravity. As we have seen, he spoke out vehemently on the Onderdonk and Griswold affairs; he penned similar editorial protests against Alonzo Potter, a New York Episcopalian who decried French novels, and against George Washington Doane, a High Church bishop involved in a fraud case. His novel *Memoirs of a Preacher* and its sequel *The Man with the Mask* were based on the life of the Rev. J. N. Maffitt, an Elmer Gantry of the time. As a whole, Lippard wrote, the nineteenth-century American ministry was beset by elitism, bigotry, and especially by "SENSUALISM and FANATICISM."[4]

In his fiction Lippard extensively satirized both historical and contemporary corruptions of Christianity. In *The Ladye Annabel* the wizard Aldarin stresses that the "Simple religion" of the Golden Rule has throughout history been "enshrouded . . . with a multitude of cumbrous falsehoods" and sullied by "Popes, priests, and monks, who say by their deeds, We do unto others as we would not have them do unto us."[5] The central satirical image of *Paul Ardenheim* is a lead crucifix made by a medieval artisan and passed down through generations to eighteenth-century Americans. The artisan, incarcerated for ten years for his heretical religious beliefs, had been promised freedom upon completion of an icon for the Church. Instead of the anticipated gold crucifix, the prisoner produced a leaden figure of a stooped, scowling Christ representing "HIM—not as he appears in the Bible, the friend of the oppressed, the Redeemer of the Poor—but as He *is* in your Church, a Sullen Spectre . . . imprisoned in the hollow forms, the blasphemous ritual—of your Church." Only when the Christian spirit is "no longer imprisoned by creeds," the artist says, "shall the Lead become Gold, and the Sneer be changed into a Smile."[6] In *Adonai* Lippard has the spirits of his Christian protagonists travel through the Middle Ages and the Reformation to point up the shortcomings of medieval Catholicism, Lutheranism, and Calvinism, and then he creates a montage in which the pilgrims witness a huge iron sepulcher, containing the body of the Lord, guarded by priests and preachers who beat back onrushing poor people who are trying to tear open the sepulcher and liberate the imprisoned Christ.

In his urban fiction Lippard put aside such metaphoric satire and directly attacked various brands of nineteenth-century religion. His most comprehensive satire on contemporary faith occurs in *The Quaker City.* Monk Hall, the monastery turned house of revel with its deep basement where corpses are thrown, harks back to Maria Monk's Hotel Dieu nunnery and other convents of nativist fiction. The overseer of Monk Hall, Devil-Bug, seems a monstrous version of the leering priest of nativist novels, while his helper, Long-haired Bess, is like a bedraggled abbess luring young novitiates into sin. While exploiting nativist devices, Lippard overturns them, for the villains of *The Quaker City* are not Catholics but various types of Protestants. Among those who revel nightly in Monk Hall are church-goers "with round faces and gouty hands, whose voices, now shouting the drinking song had re-echoed the prayer and the psalm in the aristocratic church, not longer than a Sunday ago."[7] Also present are members of " 'Bible Societies,' 'Tract Societies,' and 'Send Flannel-to-the-South-Sea Islanders Societies,' " as well as those who read "a tale from the German on *Transcendental Essences*" (pp. 48; 50).

Lippard's most colorful caricature of contemporary Protestantism is the Rev. F. A. T. Pyne (fat pine burns easily). A constant guest at Monk Hall, Pyne is a curious amalgam of evangelical enthusiast, Calvinist doomsayer, nativist Catholic-baiter, and unbridled debauchee. Pyne has "a red, round face, with thick lips, watery grey eyes, and lanky hair, of a doubtful color" forming "the details of a countenance very sanctimonious and somewhat sensual in its slightest expression" (171). A Protestant of "the Universal American Patent-Gospel School," Pyne preaches "fire and brimstone and abuse o' the Pope o' Rome" and organizes tract campaigns to convert the heathen abroad and the Pope himself, all the while ignoring the poor at home and sneaking nightly into Monk Hall to enjoy brandy, opium, and women (223, 221). One night Pyne tries to seduce the young Mabel, arguing in "a tone of spermaceti smoothness" that she is his long-lost daughter who needs fatherly comfort (229). When this ploy fails, he drugs her and is on the verge of ravishing her when Devil-Bug enters, ties the preacher to the bed crucifixion-style, and tickle-tortures him until "he blasphemed the name of his God, then invoked all the curses of hell upon his head" as "the white foam frothed around his lips" (279). Snickering at this "very corpulent representative of St. Andrew's cross," Devil-Bug exclaims, " 'Guess I got yo' on the anxious bench that time!' " (276, 277).

In his next city novel, *The Nazarene,* Lippard intensified the satire on Calvinists and nativists through his scathing portrait of Calvin Wolfe, the leader of an anti-Catholic organization who believes that *"whatever crime he may commit, whatever blasphemy he may enact, yet still he cannot sin, for he is one of the Elect of God."*[8] Wolfe praises the Native American riots of 1844 and urges his Holy Protestant League to stir up similar riots in an effort "to crush the vagabond foreigners, the idolatrous Catholics, who darken our shores like the locusts of Egypt" (127). The members of the Holy Protestant League, strict Calvinists with names like MacHowl, Bomb, and Blowhard, distribute scabrous novels whose main theme is that "Rome is the father of lies, the Pope is the Devil, and every Papist is an Idolator, a Traitor, and a Dog" (123). Wolfe declares that his "Great Party" will not only fight Catholics to the death but also will enter politics and "elect every officer from a Constable to the President" (127, 129).

Although Lippard's ardent sympathy for Catholic victims of nativist agitation lasted until the end of his life, his late novel *New York* reflects his growing fear of a Catholic conspiracy to make Washington a satellite of the Vatican City, to rid the schools of Protestant Bibles, and to establish a frontier empire in America. Distinguishing between such tolerant Catholics as Fenelon and Pascal and such persecutors as Richelieu, Lippard in this novel characterizes a New York prelate as "an ambitious atheist, a Borgia without his lust, a Richelieu with all of Richelieu's cunning, and not half of Richelieu's intellect," a "gladiator of controversy, always itching for a fight, never so happy as when he set honest men to clutching each other by the throat."[9] Instead of fearing nativist organizations, the prelate condones and supports them, for he feels that they create a disruptive atmosphere conducive to the Catholic church's scheme to divide and conquer America.

Continually attentive to the Catholic issue, Lippard also sustained the satire on private Protestant corruption that he had begun in *The Quaker City.* In *The Empire City* Lippard asks, "Who can number the innocent women who have been hurled into infamy by the same hands which were wont to grasp the sacramental cup?," asserting that *"Hell is paved with the skulls of unfaithful ministers."*[10] To illustrate this idea, Lippard in his late city novels fashioned preacher characters—the Millerite Edmund Jervis of *Memoirs of a Preacher,* the Anglican Herman Barnhurst of *The Empire City,* and the Calvinist Dr. Bulgin of *New York*— who use slick oratorical persuasion and superficial sanctity to seduce women and dupe men. Edmund Jervis is a popular preacher "who has given all the women in town love powders, and who frightens our most respectable merchants into fits, with his sermons."[11] We not only witness Jervis hypnotizing Fanny Jones with the aim of raping her, but we learn that he has ruined another young woman by marrying her and then abandoning her after publishing a false report that she was an adulterous harlot. Equally depraved is Herman Barnhurst, an oily Trinity Church minister who rants about theology and denounces infidels yet seduces a runaway girl and then delivers her to a New York whorehouse. Dr. Bulgin is a learned Calvinist theologian who looks upon the ministry as "a piece of convenient clock-work, invented some years ago, for the purpose of supplying the masses with *something to believe*; and men like himself, with a good salary, a fine house, plenty to eat and drink, fair social position, and free opportunity for the gratification of every appetite."[12]

In light of the persistence of Lippard's satire on historical and contemporary Christianity, one might think him incapable of making a positive religious reconstruction. But unlike other popular novelists such as Ned Buntline and George Foster, whose city novels focused solely on ministerial depravity, Lippard ranged through a wide array of religious and philosophical currents in an effort to fashion an eclectic faith that stood outside of church and creed. The religious figures Lippard praised by name—John Wesley, William Penn, the early Pennsylvania pietists, the Boston Unitarians, Thomas Stockton, John M'Clintock, Henry Ward Beecher—were linked by a valuation of nondogmatic, hopeful religion and a rejection of enigmatic, tyrannical Christianity.

Lippard's seemingly incongruous combination of fierce satire and benign affirmation surfaces in a footnote in *The Quaker City* in which he explains that he "has a fixed love and reverential awe" for "the religion of Jesus Christ" but only "the most intolerable disgust and loathing" for "the imposture and trickery of various copies of Simon Magus, . . . whether they take the shape of ranting Millerites, intemperate Temperance lecturers, or Reverend politicians."[13] The combination appears more frequently in delineations of terror and perversity that paradoxically lead to positive religious statements. Like some of Flannery O'Connor's stories, Lippard's novels are often so forcefully negating that the negation itself evokes a religious perception of reality.

Hostile to easily optimistic religious novelists who purveyed what he called literary "Lollypop-itude," Lippard balanced his portraits of outwardly pious but inwardly corrupt clergymen with depictions of amoral monsters who eventually see God and save the distresed. Devil-Bug, for all his fiendishness, turns out to be the main agent of retribution in *The Quaker City*; he punishes the hypocritical F. A. T. Pyne, intervenes when Luke Harvey is demanding sexual favors of Dora Livingstone, and several times saves the imperiled Mabel. Unlike his callously immoral guests, Devil-Bug comes to recognize the wages of sin. Not only is he haunted by the ghosts of his murdered victims, but he has the most ecstatic religious experience in the novel, feeling that "he, Devil-Bug the outcast of earth, the incarnate outlaw of hell, had one friend in the wide universe; that friend his Creator" (287). Similarly, Long-haired Bess, the procuress bent on ruining young women, eventually decides to help Mary and Mabel escape from Monk Hall. Lippard notes that Bess "was degraded, steeped to the very lips in pollution, cankered to the heart with loathsome vice, yet at that moment, she was a holy thing in the sight of the angels, . . . before the altar of the Almighty God" (293). Other perverse characters in Lippard's fiction who function affirmatively include the hedonistic Ravoni of *The Quaker City,* the crazed wizard Aldarin of *The Ladye Annabel,* the alchemist Isaac Van Behme of *Paul Ardenheim,* and the bloodthirsty patriots of the Revolutionary legends.

Contemporary critics were sometimes puzzled by this linkage of horror and inspiration. In the words of A. J. H. Duganne: "There is a bright, though ever-deviating thread of silvery light winding everywhere through our author's conceptions. We catch glimpses of it while wallowing in a very slough of despond into which he has led us: we follow it, attempt to trace it, and then the next moment plunge again to the mire, or tangled thicket, or vile bagnio of a prurient, morbid, and unnatural taste. Up and down, with the most perplexing sinuosities, we seek to track this line of light, till we are tired of the chase, retracing, as we eternally do, our own steps."[14] The "perplexing sinuosities" of Lippard's religion reflected a mind so repelled by bogus institutional religion that honest perversity at times seemed preferable to sham piety.

The thread of silvery light that Duganne saw in Lippard's fiction was particularly visible in moments when Lippard temporarily suspended horror on behalf of sentimental consolation. In his attempt to detach religion from cold doctrine and plant it in human feeling, he frequently equated faith with domestic emotion. Devil-Bug waxes pious and heroic when he learns that Mabel is his daughter. Elsewhere in *The Quaker City* Lippard explains that true prayer is "the whispering of the young mother, over her first-born," or "the trembling supplication of the father, by the bedside of his dying daughter"—in short, "the holiest feelings of the heart" and the "warm uprisings of man's better nature."[15] In *Memoirs of a Preacher* Lippard calls home "the holiest altar which God has reared upon the face of the earth," better than "all the Churches in the world."[16] In an essay in *The White Banner* Lippard writes: "Marriage is Religion. The love of husband and wife is Religion. The affection of brother and sister is Religion. . . . Note-shaving is not Religion."[17]

While Duganne lamented that such piety was frustratingly scarce in Lippard's fiction, other critics found it pervasive. We have seen how the *Saturday Evening Post* denounced Lippard for embroidering licentiousness with "namby-pamby sentimentalities." Similarly, Thompson Westcott charged that "every incident" in a typical Lippard novel "was surrounded with an air of prurient libertinism, yet an affectation of morality suppurated in every chapter, and a discharge of ulcerous piety pervaded every line," like a "summer ham," rank at the bone, that emitted "a faint, sweetish aroma of corruption that disgusted good taste."[18]

Westcott's complaint had some truth to it, for Lippard's sentimentality often led him to mawkish extremes, although his piety differed from that of the domestic sentimental novelists of the day because it was linked not only with violence and perversity but also with social reform. Lippard's Christianity was simple and emotional yet at the same time militant and activist. Lippard has a character in *New York* describe the Bible as "'a Democratic book, . . . so simple and yet so strong,'" that "'has caused more revolutions, given rise to more insurrections, levelled more deadly blows at absolute authority, than all other books that have been written since the beginning of the world.'"[19] In Lippard's eyes, Jesus was a tender but mighty poor man come to redress the wrongs of the oppressed of all times. Lippard gave a new political interpretation even to the most sentimental feature of mid-nineteenth-century American religion, domestic affection. By positing the brotherhood of man under a fatherly God who would establish the kingdom of heaven on earth, he was pressing beyond familial piety toward a radical liberalism that anticipated the Christian Socialism of the late nineteenth century.

Lippard was also prophetic in his portrayals of the human Jesus and a tangible heaven. In order to connect the American Revolution and modern reform with Christ's revolt against tyranny, Lippard in *Washington and His Generals* devoted a long chapter to recreating scenes from Jesus' childhood and adulthood showing the Carpenter of Nazareth as a representative poor man "thinking of his brothers—the Brotherhood of Toil!"[20] Unlike other biblical fictionists of the day such as William Ware and Charles Beecher, Lippard described physical details of Jesus' person and gave a political coloring to biblical scenes that presaged Christian Socialist fiction. In "Jesus and the Poor" and *Adonai* Lippard took the more daring step of summoning Jesus into contemporary life. In such novels of the 1890s as William Stead's *If Christ Came to Chicago* and Edward Everett Hale's *If Christ Came to Boston* the device of Jesus reappearing to lash modern moneychangers would be familiar enough, but before 1860 it was deemed sacrilegious even by novelists who took the Socinian view that Jesus was a man rather than God. In "Jesus and the Poor" Jesus appears first as a disembodied Face hovering over Girard College and Philadelphia tenements, and then as a ragged wanderer who walks into an aristocratic church, climbs into the pulpit, and beckons poor folk into the church as the congregation watches its Calvinist preacher build a wall of theological works to shut out the light beaming from that kindly Face. In *Adonai* Jesus appears to a dying prisoner, a poor child, and a group of modern reformers. Once again, Lippard's critics differed in their reactions to his embellishments of the Bible. While John Bell Bouton, Charles Chauncey Burr, and a reviewer in the *Sunday Mercury* said that Lippard's biblical material was among his best work, Thompson Westcott was shocked that Lippard "took the great Head of the Christian Church himself, and, after humanising him after his own fashion, placed a cap and bells upon his Inspiration, and then called upon the world to admire how much he did him reverence."[21]

In his treatment of the afterlife and visions of spirits Lippard was less iconoclastic than he was in his biblical fiction, for since the 1790s American writers of visionary fiction had been depicting heaven and spirits with increasing frequency and boldness. Like other visionary writers, Lippard created several fictional scenes assuring readers that heaven was not ineffably distant but rather familiar and earthlike. A dying woman in *The Nazarene* envisions herself and her mother meeting angels and even God himself in heaven. For the visionary protagonist of *Paul Ardenheim* the air is "crowded with . . . Spirit People of many tongues, tribes and forms" with whom he regularly converses.[22] In "The Heart-Broken" Lippard has Charles Brockden Brown, in the last stages of consumption, exclaim to his wife, "'I am looking into Heaven!,'" and in *New York* he has a character assure a dying man that "'we shall meet, we shall know, we shall love [our old friends] in the next world, as certainly as we ever met, knew and loved them in this.'"[23]

In such passages Lippard sounds like a number of popular writers of his day who were preparing the way for the familiar descriptions of heaven by Elizabeth Phelps Ward and others of the *Gates Ajar* school after the Civil War. However, in *Adonai* Lippard did bring innovations to the visionary mode. "Adonai" is the Hebrew word for God, so in his central character Lippard creates an anthropomorphic deity walking the earth to record mankind's foibles and virtues. In addition, Lippard resurrects the spirits of Jesus, George Washington, and America's Founding Fathers, and in a chapter called "The Darkened Glass" he draws an unusually detailed picture of the afterlife:

Not vague, nor transitory, is the life of the Other World. It is no dream, but a reality . . . And . . . we gain a vision—rather a clear sight—not so much of the gorgeous complete of Eternity, as of some single home of the Other World—some home, where live as in our world, men and women and children. . . . [O]ur hands are grasped by hands, that we thought long ago chilled by Death, forgetting that

[in] *God's universe there is no such thing as death*; but in its place, only a transition from one life or state of life to another.[24]

Lippard's experimentation with new visionary devices in *Adonai* resulted mainly from his growing interest in spiritualism. In 1851 Lippard visited the spiritualist Leah Fish and her younger sisters Maggie and Katie Fox, the renowned "spirit rappers" of Rochester. He wrote "The Darkened Glass" while in a spiritualist trance. Bouton says that in his last years Lippard constantly talked with deceased companions and had visions of his wife's spirit. He once interrupted a conversation with a friend by leaping up from his chair, pointing into the air, and exclaiming, "There is a figure in a shroud there! It is always behind me!"[25] Unlike his friend Chauncey Burr, who exposed the Fox sisters as frauds, Lippard gave lectures in defense of spiritualism, including one in 1851 on "The Supernatural" in which he drew connections among biblical, Zoroastrian, Mohammedan, and modern spiritualist visions. A curious footnote to Lippard's visionary experiences is a "Spirit Message" now in the Historical Society of Pennsylvania, a scrawled communication, bearing an approximation of Lippard's signature, ostensibly sent by him after his death to a medium; Lippard reports from heaven that his longtime suspicions about the "cold, heartless, soulless, dead condition" of institutional Christianity were accurate, as he had now met in person the warm, loving Carpenter's Son who champions the downtrodden and oppressed.[26] Apparently Lippard's spirit got to know the Carpenter's Son quite well, for in 1870 a Providence publisher issued *The Historical Life of Jesus,* a book said to have been dictated by Lippard from the other world to Olive G. Pettis, a local medium.

Other current crazes that aroused Lippard's interest were astrology, mesmerism, and magnetism. In the early 1840s Lippard befriended the Philadelphia astrologer Thomas Hague, the prototype for the reader of horoscopes in *The Quaker City* who predicts the central action of the novel. Although astrologers also figure in *The Ladye Annabel* and *Washington and His Generals,* Lippard was less interested in the reading of stars than in mind-control. He claimed that as an adolescent he had been hyponotized by

Eliphalet Nott, the president of Union College, and several of his fictional characters are either mesmerists or people placed for long periods in hypnotic trances. Lippard's main wizard characters—Aldarin, Ravoni, Isaac Van Behme—all discover in mesmerism a means of demonstrating the power of the human will. Magnetism, a pseudoscientific refinement of mesmerism positing the mental control of the electrical impulses of another's brain, intrigued Lippard in the late 1840s because it seemed to offer "a platform on which Reason and Faith may meet in concord."[27] Interpreting magnetism as "the operation of Mind upon Matter," Lippard declared that through mind-control "may be cured, or at least alleviated, one half of the diseases which afflict the human organization" (67).

Lippard's belief in the power of the will also appeared in his endorsement of heroic activity. In several novels he exaggerated the Arminian strain of the Methodism of his childhood to forge a tough assertion of human capabilites and a claim that "God is best praised by a prayer of deeds."[28] In *Washington and His Generals* this heroic Arminianism is exhibited not only by Washington's soldiers but also by the "brave . . . Preacher-Heroes of the Revolution, . . . whose hands grasped a Bible, a cross, and a sword."[29] Elsewhere in the same volume it appears in a Quaker who risks his life to save wounded in battle, an action "worth all the ages of controversial Divinity" that "sanctifies humanity, and makes us dream of men of mortal mould raised to the majesty of Gods" (55).

All of Lippard's alternatives to traditional Christianity were linked by a forceful rejection of theology. Repelled above all else by logical exposition of doctrine, Lippard regarded fiction as the age's most appropriate weapon against dogma. He sometimes couched his complaints about the orthodox sermon arrangement of text, exposition, and proof in humorously parodic terms. In "The Spermaceti Papers" for the *Citizen Soldier* he included a mock sermon on "Fatness" in which the doctrinally precise Rev. Rumpus Grizzle expounds upon "1st. Fatness *as* fatness. 2d. Fatness *as* Spermaceti. 3d. Fatness considered in relation to Ham."[30] Six years later in the *Quaker City* weekly, in a satirical

answer to attacks on his fiction, he sketched the outline for a
sham sermon of his own in which he "proved" that man is totally
depraved, that the novelist is the cause of all sin, and that mankind should continue to be divided into sects that hate each other
as much as they all hate novelists.[31]

But Lippard ususally took the defense of fiction quite seriously.
When Alonzo Potter damned Eugene Sue's fiction as immoral,
Lippard retorted that Sue's novels expressed truth more forcefully
"than ten thousand Diocesan sermons."[32] Similarly, he argued
that in Brockden Brown's novels one could learn more about "the
immortality of the soul, the paternal goodness of the Creator"
than he could "in his Mother's old Bible."[33] His longest reply
to critics of fiction appears in a digressive chapter in *Memoirs of
a Preacher* where he insists that "the Writer of novels" does "a
braver, better work for Humanity, than the pen which merely
writes a Sermon in defence of a mere creed, or turns ink into gall
again, by putting down on pure white paper, some horrible
Dogma of Theology, stolen from the cells of Heathen barbar-
ity."[34] Lippard enforced this fundamentally antitheological interpretation of fiction by writing novels that stylistically were on
the opposite end of the literary spectrum from the logical orthodox
sermon, novels whose studied unpredictability mocked the staid
consequentiality of the rigid doctrines Lippard disliked so
intensely.

Darkness below the Light: Visions of Nothingness

The marked eclecticism of Lippard's faith betrayed his restless
search for a religious certainty that always seemed just beyond
his grasp. Hawthorne's famous comment about Melville—that
he was incapable of belief yet uncomfortable in his disbelief—
was to a great extent true of Lippard. Protestantism, Lippard
stated flatly in an essay in *The White Banner,* was a failure because
it had spawned hundreds of warring sects and incompatible doctrines. Surveying "the wilderness" of Protestantism, Lippard saw
only "a sad, a hopeless, a dismal picture" where "doubt reigns"
and "chaos seems eternal."[35] Catholicism, that "mysteriously
beautiful Alp of the Past," offered refuge from "the sterile strife

of Protestantism," but it was spoiled by excessive rituals and forms (137). "Catholicism may die out and Protestantism die out, but HUMANITY will live," Lippard wrote. "The forms of the Catholic Church may fade, and the negations and abstractions of the Protestant Church may die, but Humanity will live" (138).

Placing humanity at the center of faith, Lippard verged on denying the validity of any religion by stripping away supernatural sanctions for belief. Extolling domestic sentiment, the human Jesus, magnetism, and heroic action, he retrieved religion from doubtful metaphysical realms and planted it firmly in the physical world, just as through visions of a tangible heaven or deceased friends he tried to eradicate the ineffability and otherness of the afterlife. Much of the interest of Lippard's fiction lies in his strategies for avoiding the shattering recognition that God and heaven do not exist, that religious truth is an illusion, that man is alone in an unstable world with nothing to expect after death but oblivion.

One such strategy of evasion was to voice cynical views through characters who were somehow flawed and whom Lippard could retributively punish. At the beginning of *The Quaker City* the rake Gus Lorrimer asks, " 'Life? What is it? . . . To day a jolly carousal in an oyster cellar, to-morrow a nice little pic nic in a grave-yard. One moment you gather the apple, the next it is ashes. . . . A bundle of hopes and fears, deceits and confidences, joys and miseries, strapped to a fellow's back like Pedlar's wares.' "[36] All the gloomier features of Lippard's fiction—the innumerable deceitful characters, the gore and violence, the fierce rejection of conventional faith—suggest that Lorrimer here is stating Lippard's fundamental view of life. But to avoid fully confronting this potentially nihilistic outlook, Lippard expresses it through a seducer of sisters whom he can later kill off with impunity.

This evasive tactic is equally apparent in Lippard's portrayal of Devil-Bug and Ravoni. Lippard introduces Devil-Bug as a "deplorable monstrosity, who knew no God, feared no devil, whose existence was one instinctive impulse of cruelty and bloodshed," later reiterating, "For him there had never been a church, a Bible, or a God!" (92, 189). Instead of permitting his portrait of Devil-Bug to develop into a consistently penetrating study of amoralism and atheism, Lippard for several chapters gleefully records the fiendish activity of his monster and then recoils to the secure level of sentimental piety, making Devil-Bug emerge as a heroic and self-punishing figure. Just after the most gruesome scene in the book—the dashing out of the old woman's brains—Lippard abruptly infuses remorse and religiosity into the previously callous Devil-Bug, who cries, "'I do begin to b'lieve that there is a hell!'" and who says after discovering his long-lost daughter, "'I do believe there is—a God—that's a fact!' " (205, 206). In his depiction of the priest Ravoni Lippard advances a death-of-God humanism in some ways akin to twentieth-century existentialism. Ravoni directly says, "'There is no God. There is no Heaven. There is no Hell'" (359). In horrifying contemplation of death, Ravoni exclaims: "'All black, dull, dead! Vacant space, darkness, nothingness. . . . Annihilation! . . . An awful scene of Eternal Nothingness'" (457). Ravoni calls for a "'new faith. . . in the name of MAN and for the good of MAN,'" a faith that replaces God and heaven with social reform, hedonism, and magnetism (379). Lippard here fashions a secular faith on the ruins of a supernatural one, but he distances himself from Ravoni's atheism by presenting the wizard as an intriguing but flawed fanatic whose excesses lead to a deserved death.

Lippard raises the question of God's existence with telling frequency in his fiction, and his search for answers to this question betrays his desperate need for consolation in the face of annihilating ambiguity. In *Memoirs of a Preacher* he depicts the scientist Reuben Gatherwood as an atheistic misanthrope and the preacher Edmund Jervis as a sensualist who at one point asks aloud three times, "'Is there a God?'"[37] Only when the young Fanny Jones travels into the afterlife while in a hypnotic trance does Lippard suggest that Jervis's question can be answered affirmatively. For Malachi Ham of *The Nazarene* "there is neither God, nor angel . . . to love and fear. . . . There is no future; only this worthless, wretched, present time, wherein we can only eat, drink, and die."[38] Ham is surrounded by materialists and hypocrites, and only through a vignette of a praying Catholic girl envisioning the faces of Jesus and Mary does Lippard make any kind of positive religious statement. The preacher characters of Lippard's late New York novels, Herman Barnhurst and Dr. Bulgin, are both atheists who believe that "beyond this world there [is] NOTHING."[39] When a dying man asks Barnhurst whether in death we merely "sleep and rot, rot and sleep," the preacher remains silent; only the lachrymose outcry of a young boy assures the man that "'there is something beyond the grave. There is a God! There is a heaven and a hell'" (102). The most cynical figure in Lippard's fiction, the Executioner in *Adonai,* gives long speeches emphasizing the bewildering complexity of life and the hopelessness of human effort; only the brief appearance of Jesus at the end of the book makes the Executioner disappear.

Lippard's use of such rhetorical devices to allay doubts about otherworldly belief struck some reviewers as sacrilegious and trivializing. Thompson Westcott declared, for instance, that Lippard "handled the most solemn mysteries of our religion with a flippancy that bordered on blasphemy, so that it was difficult to tell where respect ended and contempt began."[40] Lippard was indeed contemptuous of revealed faith as it was normally understood, but his underlying attitude toward religion was closer to anxiety than to flippancy. Lippard was painfully aware of the devastating attacks upon Christianity made by eighteenth-century materialists and deists, and his humanistic reconstructions of faith were often pointed directly at the likes of Voltaire and Paine. In *Washington and His Generals* Lippard answers skepticism with sentimental aestheticism, arguing that "if the Bible is a fable, it is a fable more beautiful than all the iron-hearted sophistry of your cold-blooded Philosophers"; through its "appeals to your imagination with its images of divine loveliness," it preaches a "Religion of the heart" that cannot "die of a single Voltaire or Paine."[41] In the central religious passage in *The Quaker City,* Lippard declares that if warm domestic affection is not prayer, "then let us shut the Bible and cry with the madman-atheist of France, 'There is no God—Death is an eternal sleep!'"[42]

Thus, frightened by the metaphysical implications of eight-eenth-century skepticism, Lippard sought refuge in nineteenth-century sentimentalism. His view of fiction as the best mode for political and religious discussion seems to have sprung not only from his repugnance for intellectual theology but also from his fear of skeptical attacks on faith. In this context, William Elder's "Fiction," an essay that Lippard printed in the *Quaker City* weekly in 1849, is instructive. Elder states explicitly the use of fiction as a shield against doubt that is implicit in much of Lippard's work. Elder confesses to having been devastated by reading essays attacking Christianity by Voltaire, Hume, and the British deists: "When I found that these conjurors had succeeded in nothing but discrediting universal experience, reducing faith to a phantasm, sense to delusion, and turning the good old universe out of doors, I felt free to look elsewhere for something to live on." With traditional religion no longer an option, Elder turned to "the children and the priests of nature, . . . the novelists," whom he welcomed "with as hearty cheer as if they came in the rough garment and leathern girdle of the old time Seers." Above all, Elder explained, fiction was valuable for "delineating humanity as it is and may be."[43]

Like Elder, Lippard discovered in fiction a means of turning away from insoluble otherworldly issues to humanity. Fiction for Lippard became a rhetorical tool for buttressing the credibility of secular replacements for revealed faith without risking the potentially destructive outcome of philosophical exposition. In using fiction for religious discussion Lippard was not alone in his day. Elder's passing remark that "even Sunday School libraries have their proportion of fictitious narrative" is borne out by the fact that in Lippard's lifetime the major American religious publishing houses were making a wholesale shift from theological to story tracts.[44] At the same time, a good number of American novelists—Catherine Sedgwick, Lydia Maria Child, Sylvester Judd, Fanny Fern, Maria Cummins, Joseph Holt Ingraham—were independently producing popular religious fiction. In most cases, these writers, like Lippard, were driven to write novels as a result of repugnance to theology and fear of philosophy.

There are, however, important differences between Lippard and these other "priests of nature." The differences become apparent when we summarize Lippard's religious views as they appear in his fiction: institutional Christianity is a failure, its ministers often venal and licentious; there is evidence that the Bible is fabulous and God and afterlife nonexistent; men generally are caught up in a tangled web of hypocrisy, bestiality, and sexual perversity; quite possibly life is meaningless and truth illusory; to avoid being paralyzed by this terrifying outlook, we may direct our attention to such tangible or visible things as domestic sentiment, social religion, the human Jesus, familiar views of an earthlike heaven, heroic or moral behavior, and an aesthetic reading of the Bible. The novels of other pious authors of the day generally left out the first four steps of this religious quest, turning at once to those consolingly secular alternatives to otherworldly faith that Lippard embraced only after shattering explorations of amorality and atheism. The typical Lippard novel may place us in the soft armchair of sentiment, but not until it has held us dangling for long periods over the abyss of doubt.

Chapter Five
Lippard in the Literary Community

As a literary critic and as a novelist, Lippard was in the curious position of a writer for the masses who nevertheless sought to distinguish himself from other popular writers of the day and to place himself in the select group of Americans who were trying to forge a distinct national literature. In one sense, Lippard was the epitome—almost the caricature—of the popular writer: he dismissed accepted rules of literary art and denigrated established critics; he advanced democratic social and religious views in sensational tales that appealed to a lowbrow taste; the publishing history of his serial novels reflected a new phenomenon in American literary merchandizing—the mass production of cheap paper-covered works designed for immediate consumption by an increasingly mobile readership.

On the other hand, Lippard often expressed attitudes akin to those of major authors of the American Renaissance. Like Poe and Hawthorne, he pointedly attacked the facile optimism and shallow morality of typical popular fiction of the period. Like Melville he wrote big, sometimes cumbersome novels that challenged social convention by exposing man's hypocrisy and deceit, and like Emerson he vigorously rejected historical Christianity on behalf of an inspirational outlook distant from dogma. Despite his deep sympathy for the mass audience, Lippard explored unconventional themes atypical of popular literature in antebellum America.

Lippard as Literary Critic

This, Lippard wrote in 1844, is "The Crippled Age of American Literature," a time when the average American author is
"part beggar, part cripple, and part thief." Lippard asked, "Oh,
is it not a burning shame that a land which has given birth to
men like Charles Brockden Brown, J. Fenimore Cooper, W. G.
Simms, Washington Irving, N. P. Willis, Edgar A. Poe—a land
which is everlastingly boasting of its wisdom, its freedom, its
greatness—should raise a colossal pillar, high over all its insti-
tutions, and perch on that pillar's capital a leprous beggar, whom
it worships as the—God help us—the Incarnation of American
Literature."[1]

Especially diseased, in Lippard's eyes, was the domestic fiction
of the day and the prettified prose and poetry that was appearing
in such magazines as *Graham's,* the *Casket,* and *Godey's Lady's
Book.* Recent scholars who have argued that mid-nineteenth-century popular fiction, in its enfeebling sentimentality, sped "the
feminization of American culture" risk oversimplification by ignoring a figure like Lippard, a very popular writer who, despite
sentimental tendencies of his own, regularly denounced the literary pablum he believed was being spoon-fed to the American
public.[2]

Like his friend Poe, Lippard early in his career burlesqued lesser
authors. In "The Sanguine Poetaster" and "The Bread Crust Papers" for the *Spirit of the Times,* Lippard parodied the empty and
overblown verses of Henry B. Hirst ("Henry Bread Crust") and
Thomas Dunn English ("Thomas Done Brown"), two Philadelphia poets. Bread Crust, a stammering dandy with vapid blue
eyes, thin white eyebrows, and a bland complexion, woos the
wealthy Emeline W—— by reading her his "Cwab Twee and
Old Gway," a farcically bad nature poem that induces Emeline
to dismiss him from her home. He gets some of his own medicine
when he is rousted out of bed in the middle of the night by Done
Brown, who has come to show off "The Ocean Shore," a Spen-
serian piece he has been working on for a year. "It was a good
poem," Lippard tells us. "Such a mingling of invocations to this
or that muse, with such descriptions of sun-sets, or this or that

sea shore, such great big words, dragged neck-and-heels into the service of poor, weak, sickly, consumptive ideas, and such graphic portraitures of fairy islands, . . . frequently visited by angels. . . . It was a very grand poem."[3] Bread Crust and Done Brown compete for the affections of the soft-brained Angeline Smivers by reading flowery love poems to her and then arranging a duel at which the cowardly Done Brown fails to appear.

"The Sanguine Poetaster" and "The Bread Crust Papers" were not only popular but also were imitated by other critics of the period: Poe borrowed from Lippard the pejorative name "Done Brown" in a scathing review of Thomas Dunn English, and Thompson Westcott used both "Done Brown" and "Bread Crust" in his witty overview of current literature for the *Sunday Dispatch,* "Philadelphia and the Philadelphians in 1850." In the meantime, after quitting the *Spirit of the Times* Lippard continued to lampoon the precious, pretentious writing of popular sentimental authors. In an essay on American literature in the *Citizen Soldier,* Lippard, noting the "mingled imbecility, pseudo-morality, and . . . positive trash" of contemporary magazine literature, declared: "WE DO PROTEST . . . against the glaring absurdity of calling these periodicals American Literature" and "against the prevalence of the petticoat" in "the emasculated productions" of "these hermaphroditical pamphlets."[4]

In his most famous literary columns for the *Citizen Soldier,* "The Spermaceti Papers" and "The Walnut Coffin Papers," Lippard dramatized this protest by satirizing the mawkish material produced by Philadelphia's leading periodical publishing firm, George R. Graham and Company. Repelled by the tendency of such Graham authors as Charles J. Peterson to hide behind numerous male and female pseudonyms, Lippard has the poet Professor Peter Sun, who possesses "a genius, that can wear pants to-day and petticoats to-morrow," announce to his coworkers on the *Universal Lamp-post and Saturday Stick:* "'I'll be a list of 'Distinguished American Contributors' myself. I'll write under a dozen names. I'll be any quantity of modest young ladies—nice young gentlemen—celebrated authors.'"[5] Sun, whose finest poem is "The Pap Spoon—A Pollywogue," is "the father of the

bombazine school of literature," which is "fragrant of the petticoat, . . . speaks much of the female influence, and plunges
neck-and-heels into the sentimental" (CS, July 19, 1843). The
Rev. Rumpus Grizzle (Rufus Griswold), the literary critic for the
Universal Lamp-post, praises Sun and other effeminate writers while
aspersing solid authors such as Poe; Grizzle lays plans for his own
"'great yaller kivered pamphlet, with all sorts of nice plates o'
young ladies a nursin' babies, little pussies playin' with spools
o' cotton, and pictures o' cross-eyed poets'" (CS, September 20,
1843).

Lippard incorporated his protest against popular sentimentalism in his best-known novel, The Quaker City. Through his portrayal of Sylvester J. Petriken, the foppish editor of the Ladies'
Western Hemisphere and Continental Organ who regales his Monk
Hall companions with readings of saccharine moral verse, Lippard
sustains the satire on periodical writers he began in his columns
for the Spirit of the Times and the Citizen Soldier. His longest attack
on the sentimentalists appears in a digressive introduction to a
gloomy chapter, "The Pit of Monk Hall," in which Devil-Bug
carries a body into his dark cellar. Lippard warns the "sweet
maiden-man" author to pass by the chapter to avoid an irreparable
wounding of his delicate sensibility. Lippard writes: "Soft maker
of verses so utterly blank, that a single original idea never mars
their consistent nothingness, penner of paragraphs so daintily
perfumed with quaint phrases and stilted nonsense, we do not
want you here." We delight, Lippard says, to picture the "phan-
toms," the "nightmares," "the terrible chaos of a heart and soul
like those of Devil-Bug":

> But as for you, sweet virgin man, oh reign forever the Prince of
> Syllabub and Lollypop! And when you are dead, should we survive your
> loss, we'll raise above your grave a monument of deep regard for your
> money. Darley shall do the design. A be-pantalooned girl, with a
> smooth face and wiry hair, sitting on a volume of travels, with a bundle
> of blank verses in one hand and a cake-basket full of paragraphs in the
> other. It shall be modelled in syllabub, dear Mister-Miss, surrounded
> with a border of sugar plums, besprinkled with pendant drops of frozen
> treacle. The foundation of the monument shall be of gingerbread; the

crest, a rampant Katy-did. The motto . . . shall be—"Here lies the Poet of Twaddle-dom, whose whole life was characterized by a pervading vein of Lollypop-itude." This is our promise, sweet maiden-man; therefore we pri-thee pass this chapter by![6]

While establishing himself as a determined critic of "feminized" literature, Lippard also lamented a sheepish obsequiousness to foreign literary models on the part of many American authors. Shocked by the excessive adulation lavished on the visiting Charles Dickens in 1842, Lippard in the *Spirit of the Times* noted that Dickens was "a great man" but no "demigod" and declared: "Let us dine Boz—let us feed Boz—but do not let us lick his dish after he has eaten out of it."[7] Reporting a fictitious meeting between his police-court persona, Billy Brier, and Dickens, Lippard wrote that "we indulged in a hearty laugh at the absurd idolatry of our countrymen, and the pictures which Mr. Dickens was evidently storing away in his common-place book of American eccentricities, weaknesses, follies, and ridiculous extremes" (*CS,* March 9, 1842).

Despite his exploitation of British and Continental genres and his outspoken praise of such foreign authors as Eugene Sue, George Sand, Bulwer-Lytton, G. P. R. James, and Harrison Ainsworth, Lippard was more a manipulator than an imitator of foreign literary devices, and he emphasized the importance of originality. In response to charges that *The Quaker City* was a copy of Sue's *The Mysteries of Paris,* he insisted that his novel was "planned and partly written before the author heard of the existence of Eugene Sue. It is not, therefore, an imitation of Eugene Sue or of any other writer."[8] Deploring the derivativeness of much American fiction, Lippard in "The Spermaceti Papers" had Professor Peter Sun fear Poe's critical "tomahawk" because, in Sun's words, Poe "'knows [that] I steal my stories'" from James and Bulwer and that the typical "Original American Novel" in the *Universal Lamp-post* is in fact a plagiarism of a foreign work.[9]

Lippard's antipathy for imitative fiction derived from an intense Americanism and a confidence that indigenous soil was well suited for the cultivation of a healthy national literature. Lippard singled out a few Americans who raised themselves above sentimentality or artistic ineptitude toward a higher order of literature. In Charles Brockden Brown he discovered a partner in terror who, like himself, had abandoned a legal for a literary career, struggled against tuberculosis, and suffered neglect or condescension at the hands of most American critics. Having prefaced *The Quaker City* with a dedication to Brown, Lippard in "The Heart-Broken" (1848) reviewed Brown's life, lauded his first four novels, and argued for the removal of Brown's remains from their obscure resting-place to the fashionable Laurel Hill Cemetery. Calling Brown *"a Man of Genius, in advance of his age,"* Lippard credited him with "almost supernatural analysis of motive and character," noting in particular the "delineations of a stern and unrelenting Fanaticism" in *Wieland,* the reduction of "virtue to an enigma" in *Ormond,* the "description of the Yellow Fever of '93" in *Arthur Mervyn,* and the accounts of Indian warfare and somnabulism in *Edgar Huntly.* [10] Complaining that Brown was generally ignored in America while appreciated in England by such qualified judges as William Godwin and Bulwer-Lytton, Lippard called for renewed respect of the forgotten Philadelphia author.

An ardent defender of Brown, Lippard was less detailed and less consistently glowing in his comments on Cooper, Irving, and other major American authors. In his letter of 1844 to Cooper requesting support for his proposed magazine of American historical romance, Lippard described "how many weary hours of pain, and wrong and orphanage, have been cheered and hallowed by the perusal of 'The Pioneers,' 'The Last of the Mohicans' 'The Prairie,' 'The Spy' or 'The Red Rover' or other volumes of your numerous works." [11] Lippard wrote a dedication to Cooper in *Herbert Tracy,* praised him along with Harrison Ainsworth in a footnote in *The Quaker City,* and in 1849 confessed to feeling inspired by "the great religion of nature" in the Leatherstocking novels. [12] Lippard felt deeply betrayed, however, when Cooper late in life embraced doctrinal Episcopalianism and exaggerated his longstanding paternalistic social views. Lippard lamented the theological narrowness of Cooper's late novel, *The Sea Lions,* and when Cooper came out against homestead exemption Lippard wrote that "as a Novelist, writing for the People, his conduct is inexplicable. He is like a profane swearer, who sins every moment, without even the hope of profit for his sins" (*QCW*, April 28, 1849).

Lippard had similarly mixed feelings about Irving. Although he often placed Irving in a small group of worthy American authors, and although he attempted Irvingesque characterization in "The Monster with Three Names" and in parts of *Paul Ardenheim*, he resented Irving's preoccupation with British and Spanish subjects. The transcendentalist reformer Theodore Parker came to seem more attractive to Lippard than either Cooper or Irving; in 1849 Lippard reprinted in the *Quaker City* weekly two of Parker's essays on prison reform advancing the thesis that criminals, forced to misdeeds by poverty, are as much society's victims as its foes.

The common denominator of Lippard's evaluation of popular and major American authors was a firm dismissal of nonutilitarian literature that slighted or ignored the masses, whose cause Lippard espoused with increasing fervency. "Our Idea of a National Literature," Lippard wrote in 1849, "is simply: that a literature which does not work practically, for the advancement of social reform, . . . or which is too dignified or too good to picture the wrongs of the great mass of humanity, is just good for nothing at all" (*QCW*, February 10, 1849).

Finding in sentimental magazine literature and in the late works of Cooper and Irving a complacent acceptance of the status quo, Lippard held up certain foreign authors as worthy promoters of egalitarian radicalism. He argued that the literati of America's eastern cities who pampered Charles Dickens with feasts and awards overlooked the central fact that Dickens, as a writer for the people, could only be disgusted by aristocrats' idolatry. Similarly, he insisted that those who pilloried Eugene Sue and George Sand as immoral novelists failed to mention Sue's defense of "the Rights of Labor" and pictures of the "miseries of landless and homeless Toil," or Sand's stirring descriptions of "the shames and wrongs which her sex had suffered at the hands of a remorseless civilization."[13]

In an essay of 1849 Lippard argued that Americans had failed to develop a national literature because of divisiveness and elitism, while Europeans were far more unified in advancing the "great Idea" of "the right of Labor to its fruits, coupled with the reorganization of the social system" (*QCW*, February 10, 1849). Lippard hardly gave blanket approval to foreign literature, however. He exempted only Dickens, G. P. R. James, and Bulwer-Lytton from the charge that " 'ENGLISH NOVELS' do more to corrupt the minds of American children, than any sort of bad literature that ever cursed the world" because they are "anti-American and anti-human."[14] Lippard regretted that Bulwer left behind the "ferocious radicalism" of his early novels on behalf of a grovelling reverence for the British upper classes in his later works (149). Thackeray, in Lippard's judgment, was a cynical misanthrope, while Wordsworth changed from a champion of the common man to a conservative who "lost all faith in social redemption" (149).

Critical of authors who ignored or abandoned social reform, Lippard also denounced literary anthologists, publishers, critics, and plagiarists, all of whom he regularly characterized as mercenary exploiters of creative genius. In order to foster a sound reformist national literature, he wrote, "first we must scourge from us, the mere hucksters and trimmers of literature, the Griswolds and Headleys, the Fipples and the Pipples and all that class of people who *make* books."[15] In "The Spermaceti Papers" Lippard portrays the Grey Ham (George R. Graham) as a money-hungry publisher who flatters the rich while insulting the poor, and Rumpus Grizzle (Griswold) as a critic ready to " 'cut up' the authors—preach a little, pray a little, lie a little, and steal a little."[16] Unimpressed by the efforts of Griswold and the Boston critic Edwin Whipple to collect American prose and poetry in anthologies, Lippard regarded anthologists as leeches sucking the lifeblood of original writers. Similarly, he looked upon critics as insects and reptiles crawling over the corpse of imaginative literature, or as the venal lackeys of publishers. When one Philadelphia critic noted that Lippard was popular with the many rather than with the select, Lippard retorted: "That 'many' the rough, hardy people of the workshop and the plough; that 'select,' some dozen newspaper and magazine editors" of the eastern cities who make criticism "a mere matter of dollars and cents, . . . so much praise for so many pennies."[17] While Lippard often laughed bitterly at the urban critics who generally derogated him and brandished his acceptance by common folk, despair over his exclusion from the literary establishment sometimes darkened his defiance:

Ah, sad and bitter is the fate of the American Author.

He flashes for a moment, there—a falling meteor above the horizon of life—and then hisses down into the night, and is dark forever.

Or is he successful? Then malice hunts and envy stabs him. Hideous lizards, that crawl into slimy eminence, hiss at him as he goes by. The mercenary Press—the Libel—the Lie; these are the bloodhounds tracking every footstep of his way.[18]

In light of the harshness of Lippard's attacks on many literary figures of his day, it is not surprising that some of his contemporaries called him a hypersensitive man with an acute persecution complex. Theodore Parker noted that Lippard had "superior abilities" yet seemed "ill at ease, stung, perhaps, by misfortune or neglect."[19] Thompson Westcott wrote that Lippard—"a perfect Ishmaelite, with his hand against every man in the profession, and he himself, laboring under the delusion that every man's hand was against him"—believed "that all Christendom was in league against him. This made him malignant, despairing, reckless and vindictive. His life was one continued irresolution as to whether he should leave the world in disgust at its meanness, or kick it as long as his mental boots would stand the indignant application—whether he should cut the throat of all his earthly associations, or summarily cut his own, and end the difficulty."[20]

There is no doubt that Lippard's literary criticism was frequently colored by an emotionalism growing from personal misfortune, by a strong reaction to hostile criticism, and by a populist emphasis that often made him blind to stylistic niceties. Moreover, his sympathy for neglected or persecuted authors occasionally led him into poor judgment; for instance, he warmly praised two second-rate poets who met early deaths, the alcoholic and public opium addict John Lofland of Wilmington, and the poverty-stricken Sumner Lincoln Fairfield of Philadelphia and elsewhere. Lippard displayed verve and a good amount of wit, however, in his forays against the urban literary establishment, and his anger and vindictiveness reflected an understandable frustration over the paucity of precedent for the kind of politicized national literature he endorsed. Much popular American literature of the day was indeed mawkish and supportive of the status quo, and the major literature tended to be apolitical and only sporadically concerned with current events. If Lippard was extreme and finally unsuccessful in his attempts to scourge "maiden-men" and moneychangers from the literary temple, he can at least be credited as a bold democratic voice crying in a wilderness of sentimentalism and complacency.

Lippard and Poe

Many commentators on Lippard have been quick to link him with Poe because of biographical connections between the two writers as well as certain thematic similarities between their fiction. In 1850 Thompson Westcott jokingly exaggerated the morbid tendencies of Lippard and Poe by picturing them meeting to fabricate schemes for theatrical public suicides. In 1886 a Philadelphia newspaper recalled Lippard as "a brilliant and erratic genius, who flashed like a star in the literary firmament and whose life in many respects resembled that of Edgar Allan Poe."[21] One of the chief reasons for the perpetuation of scholarly interest in Lippard during the twentieth century has been his relationship with his more famous contemporary.

Concrete biographical evidence of this relationship is slim yet intriguing. Lippard presumably met Poe in 1842, since the offices of DuSolle's the *Spirit of the Times* was diagonally across the street from those of *Graham's Magazine,* where Poe was working at the time. Poe probably provided Lippard with information on the Graham group for "The Spermaceti Papers" in the *Citizen Soldier*; not only did Lippard mention details about the Graham operation that would have been unknown to a complete outsider, but also he singled out Poe for praise in his generally negative portrayal of the magazine company. At any rate, Poe was aware of Lippard by early 1844, when his letter evaluating *The Ladye Annabel* was published as an epilogue to *Herbert Tracy*.

Although Poe had mixed feelings about Lippard's literary abilities, he developed a loyal friendship with the younger writer, whose *Quaker City* newspaper office he visited in July 1849, when he was in desperate straits. At that time he gave Lippard a copy of *Eureka* in which Lippard later wrote, "Presented to me by Poe, when we parted, and when I saw him last."[22] Three weeks after Poe's death on October 7, 1849, Lippard in the *Quaker City* weekly noted sadly that "only a few weeks ago" Poe had come "to our office" nostalgic for Virginia and sick in body and mind. Recalling Poe's conversation about *Eureka* and about his wife, Lippard expressed sympathy for this "man of genius, hunted by the world, trampled upon by the men whom he had loaded with favors, and disappointed in every turn of life." While admitting that Poe did have faults, including a propensity to excessively harsh criticism, Lippard denied the common charge that Poe was a dissolute alcoholic, arguing that one drink would go to Poe's head and make him seem more inebriated than he really was. Lippard correctly predicted that Poe's "name will live, while three-fourths of the bastard critics and mongrel authors of the present day go down to nothingness and night."[23]

The memory of Poe haunted Lippard, who in January 1850 wrote for his newspaper an even longer report of Poe's last visit. In a vignette about the emotional meeting between "The Poet" and "The Author," Lippard recalled that Poe, wearing ragged clothes and only one shoe, had struggled up the four flights of stairs to Lippard's office and lamented that he "had no bread to eat—no place to sleep—not one friend in God's world," begging "the Author not to forsake him." Sickened by the sight of Poe reduced to poverty and loneliness, Lippard went out into the hot, cholera-ridden streets of Philadelphia to collect money but then took sick himself and had just enough strength to make it home. The next morning he returned to his printing office to find Poe slumped in a chair with his face in his hands, desperate in the

belief that Lippard had deserted him and longing to travel to
Virginia. Lippard then went out again to solicit money from old
literary acquaintances, collecting five dollars each from Louis A.
Godey and Samuel D. Peterson and unspecified sums from Charles
Chauncey Burr, John Sartain, and a Mr. Miskey, a clerk of
Sartain's.

Having relieved Poe and insured his return to Virginia, Lippard
became understandably bitter after Poe's death when suddenly
his work received fawning panegyrics from "literary hucksters
who had lied to him—booksellers who had left him to starve—
gentlemen of literature, who had seen him walk the hot streets of
Philadelphia without food or shelter." Piqued by such abrupt
praise, Lippard was also annoyed by Rufus Griswold's negative
portrait of Poe in the preface to his collected edition of Poe's
works:

> That the Poet was poor was bad enough; but that after his death
> . . . he should be edited by a fellow who he heartily despised as the
> quack of quacks—the very Brandreth of literature—and that this fellow
> should dare to talk of the "irreligion" and "malignancy" of the dead
> Poet, even while pretending to be his biographer and admirer! Verily,
> there is something worse than poverty or starvation. It is to have such
> a Quack attempt to edit your work after you are dead. (*QCW*, January
> 26, 1850)

Lippard found in Poe, as in Brockden Brown, a fellow explorer
of dark, unconventional themes and a maltreated man of genius
with whom he could identify. Early in his career Lippard distinguished Poe from other magazine writers of the day. In "The
Spermaceti Papers" he portrayed Poe as a tough-minded critic
feared by other Graham authors and vindictively underpaid by
his resentful publishers. Noting the decline in the literary quality
of *Graham's* after Poe quit his position, Lippard stressed that Poe
had given "this now weak and flimsy periodical a tone of refinement and mental vigor, which all the imbecility of its conductors
for a year past, could not entirely erase or utterly annihilate."[24]
Reviewing Poe's "Lecture on American Poetry" (1843), Lippard
called Poe "perhaps the most original writer that ever existed in

America," recognizing in Poe's works a unique mixture of ratio-
cination, terror, dream imagery, psychological depth, and humor
(*CS,* November 15, 1843). Applauding Poe's "towering fame"
as a poet, fictionist, critic, and lecturer, Lippard looked forward
to "a sound Magazine, devoted to all the higher objects of
American Literature, edited, owned, and controlled by Mr. Poe"
(*CS,* January 10, 1844). We may surmise that Lippard commis-
erated with Poe's persistent but frustrated plans for a magazine
of his own, plans which Lippard shared and which he was more
successful than his friend in implementing. No doubt Lippard
felt a personal affiliation with Poe in other ways. Both were
laborious and ordinarily rational men who suffered from inter-
mittent eruptions of melancholia, hysteria, and persecution
mania. Both were interested in mesmerism and magnetism, and
both wrote fiction that explored dream psychology, irrational
states, Gothic terror, necrophilia, and the death of beautiful
women.

There were significant differences, however, between Poe and
Lippard. Poe wished to detach fiction from the kind of political
commentary and moral preachment that Lippard called for. The
heresy of the didactic that Poe deplored was evident in much of
Lippard's writing. For Lippard fiction was a way of changing the
world; for Poe it was, to a great extent, a means of escaping it.
Whereas Poe wished to turn from the vulgarities around him
toward a timeless realm of aesthetic values, Lippard wanted to
exaggerate such vulgarities in order to expose the ugliness of
contemporary society and to emphasize the pressing need for
reform. While Poe prized autonomous literary art, Lippard believed that "literature merely considered as ART is a despicable
thing. . . . These people who talk about art, art, art, in literature are terrible twaddlers. Grace of style, elegance of language
are invaluable *aids* to literature, but they are not the *ultimates* of
literature. The great object of literature, is the social, mental and
spiritual elevation of Man. . . . True literature is only the embodiment of a true Thought."[25]

Poe and Lippard also differed in their views of the writing
process. Poe was the consummately deliberate author, patiently

and rigorously revising his works in the interest of achieving structural symmetry and singleness of effect. Believing that inspiration left to itself was naive and formless, he saw literature as the outgrowth of a cool, judicious application of intellect. Lippard, particularly during his prolific period between 1844 and 1850, often wrote in virtual fits of frenzy, frequently sending his works to press unchecked and unrevised. One of his associates, G. M. W. Geist, said that when Lippard's novels were running through the *Quaker City* weekly "he would not begin writing the weekly installment until the morning of the day before the paper had to go to press, and when he began he would not rise until his eight or ten columns were finished." Geist recalled sitting by Lippard's side, keeping his cigars lit as he puffed and wrote furiously, and taking the copy sheet by sheet to the compositors. In his rebellion against staid, logical forms of literary expression, Lippard intentionally ignored the kinds of narrative unities Poe valued so highly. At the end of one of the serial segments of *Memoirs of a Preacher* Lippard left a character, Ralph Jones, dangling from a frail strip of lattice-work outside a mansion window. When Geist asked him what he planned to do with Ralph, he replied, "I cannot tell until next week."[26] As it turned out, he wrote several chapters before bothering to remove Ralph from the lattice. Whereas Poe constantly strived for stylistic precision, Lippard was willing to sacrifice beauty and even grammar in the interest of communicating the message or the emotion. In his words, "Style is only the dress of thought. A strong man may make a bad style popular; the reader does not look at the dress, but at the form which that dress serves to clothe. A weak man may write ever so euphoniously; style, grammar, and words all correct, and the smoothest sound; and yet he can never become a popular writer."[27]

We may understand why Poe found even in *The Ladye Annabel,* a novel Lippard worked on for the relatively long period of three years, evidence of the author's tendency to be "in too desperate a hurry to give due attention to details."[28] We may also understand Westcott's comment that Lippard's words seem "to skip and leap, and go polkaising all about the nucleus of his object, throwing themselves into all kinds of queer attitudes and tossing their plumed heads to the winds."[29] Charles Chauncey Burr, seeing the "wild, heedless, reckless *dashing on*" of Lippard's prose as a sign of impassioned genius, argued: "What has he to do with *style,* whose great heart is already a furnace of fire-thoughts, seething and simmering with emotions for which he can find no utterance. Style indeed: that is a thing for pedants, word-mongers, sentence-makers to talk about."[30]

Historically, the stylistic differences between Poe and Lippard reflect distinct and lasting trends in the outlook of American writers. In his emphasis on the detachment of literature and the importance of stylistic precision, Poe articulated an attitude that would pass through Baudelaire and the art-for-art's-sake school to Ezra Pound, T. S. Eliot, and the New Critics. Lippard was as far from this current as he was from its antithesis—the realistic school that aimed at social commitment and the sober portrayal of ordinary life, exemplified by the work of William Dean Howells, Theodore Dreiser, Sinclair Lewis, and the New Journalists. In exposing social relations through passionate flights of the subversive imagination, and freely drawing on the irrational and grotesque, Lippard anticipated a third direction: the radical demystification evident in certain works by Mark Twain, Edward Bellamy, Ignatius Donnelly, Charlotte Perkins Gilman, Jack London, and H. P. Lovecraft, and developed systematically by Kafka and the surrealists.

We have no record of Poe's response to Lippard's major works—the reformist city novels—but we can guess from his judgment of Eugene Sue's *The Mysteries of Paris* that he would have found things to criticize in them. In Poe's eyes, Sue was a popular novelist bent on writing best-sellers and interested in political reform only secondarily and opportunistically. "The philosophical motives attributed to Sue are absurd in the extreme," Poe wrote. "His first, and in fact his sole object, is to make an exciting, and therefore saleable book. The cant (implied or direct) about the amelioration of society, etc., is but a very usual trick among authors, whereby they hope to add such a tone of dignity or utilitarianism to their pages as shall gild the pill of their licentiousness."[31] Lippard received similar criticism from contemporary commentators. A. J. H. Duganne, for instance, said that for all its pretensions to politicism *The Quaker City* "was written but to *sell*."[32] Poe probably would have objected to the reformist comment in the city novels because it showed Lippard not only committing the heresy of the didactic but also pandering directly to the mass audience.

For all these differences between Poe and Lippard, we should remember that Poe found *The Ladye Annabel* "richly inventive and imaginative" and that the two writers had much in common. Had Lippard as a fictionist attempted verisimilitude in the interest of advancing precise moral or political solutions to real problems in everyday life, we may surmise that Poe would have dismissed him altogether. In fact, though, Lippard hated comfortable moralism almost as much as Poe, and the religious and political didacticism of his own fiction was often complicated by an underlying recognition that there were no easy answers. Had Lippard consistently followed his own advice that literature should be controlled solely by the great idea of social reorganization, he might have produced staidly programmatic works along the lines of Theodore Parker's essays on prison reform or Charles Sheldon's novel *In His Steps*. Instead, he produced alinear novels peopled by ghouls and freaks, riddled with literal and metaphorical trap doors, novels that twisted and heaved, here making a sober political statement and there casting the reader into a black pit.

D. H. Lawrence's judgment that Poe was "an adventurer into vaults and cellars and horrible underground passages of the human soul" could be readily applied to Lippard.[33] In *The Ladye Annabel*, for example, Lippard studies the seemingly tame theme of democracy supplanting tyranny in determinedly irrational fashion, paying little attention to the political premise while exploring sadism, nightmare, and terror. In a central scene in the novel, the live burial of the prince Adrian along with the murderer Balvardo in a vault beneath a Florentine castle, Lippard reproduces frenzy in a way that recalls such Poe stories as "The Pit and the Pendulum" or "A Descent into the Maelstrom." The normally rational Adrian at first responds to his quandary coolly, searching for a spring that might open the door of the cavern. When he finds that escape is impossible, he becomes increasingly disturbed, having visions of a grinning Skeleton God and quenching his thirst by ripping open his arm and gulping his own blood. The situation is made even more hellish by the presence of Balvardo, who is burning with the pangs of starvation and thirst. Adrian soon discovers a deep well in the middle of the cavern and decides to climb down its walls to seek an escape passage. When he throws a large rock into the well to gauge its depth, he waits for a long moment and then hears a distant crash, as "up, up from the fathomless depths, thundering and shrieking, arose the deafening echoes, yelling like spirit-voices in the ear of the trembling man, as he swayed to and fro over the blackness of the void."[34] As he inches down the damp walls of the well, Adrian several times nearly loses his grip, and snakes and lizards wriggle over his hands and legs. When he at last discovers a passageway out, he wonders whether it is "a dream, a phantasmal creation of fancy, a mocking delusion of his crazed brain" (246–47). His escape through the passage only leads him to more terror, as he finds himself poised on precipitous, rocky cliffs outside the castle that tumble "a score of fathoms down . . . like the sides of one death-bowl of ebony" (248).

Like Poe, Lippard utilizes horrific settings that can be interpreted as physical emblems of irrational states. This strategy is apparent in nearly all of Lippard's novels: witness the pit below Monk Hall in *The Quaker City,* the bloody battlefields of the Revolutionary legends, the dragonlike train of *The Empire City,* the gloomy Block House and hermitage in *Paul Ardenheim,* the huge Temple in *New York,* all of which are exterior projections of the inner fears and fantasies Lippard is trying to probe. The main difference between Poe's and Lippard's treatment of the irrational is that Poe normally exploits the short-story mode to focus on a limited number of characters and settings in order to achieve singleness of effect, whereas Lippard generates tangled series of terrifying scenes in novels that point in many directions at once. Poe is the cerebral sculptor, carving the irrational with the knife of intellect, using such literary tools as the first-person narrator and self-reflective characterization, and cutting away the rough edges of moral or social commentary in the interest of artistic purity. Lippard is the emotional participant and observer, by turns leaping right into the turbulent world he has created, retreating momentarily to make a political or religious point, then jumping in a different direction altogether. Poe would probably have polished the live-burial scene in *The Ladye Annabel* by removing it from any political context and transforming it into a self-contained story illustrating the collapse of reason in the face of mental anguish and physical duress. Lippard, in contrast, not only surrounds the scene with unrelated events but also has Adrian recover from his fright sufficiently to become the democratic ruler of Florence after marrying the virtuous Annabel. While Poe typically devoted individual tales to such themes as fright in dark pits, the effects of magnetism, or the death of beautiful women, Lippard frequently gathered together all of these topics and more in sprawling novels that were light-years distant from Poe's symmetrical tales.

The Quaker City and Lippard's Literary Stature

Lippard's criticism of other writers and his relations with Poe raise larger questions about his place in American literary history. A main reason for the scholarly neglect of Lippard is his reputation as an unartistic sensationalist accepted by the masses of his day but best forgotten by the discriminating. Lippard helped to create this reputation, openly transgressing accepted rules of fictional art and courting popular favor. Not only did his novels have wide mass appeal in his own time, but after his death they continued to be identified with a lowbrow audience. *'Bel of Prairie Eden* was reprinted in 1870 as a western dime novel in DeWitt's Ten Cent Romance series, and in 1943 a first edition of *The Rose of Wissahikon* was advertised to rare book collectors as follows: "Yes, you really must read this one. Lippard was the first Grade A American out-and-out sensationalist in story writing—and this is the perfect specimen of his craft."[35]

Even if this lowbrow image told the whole story about Lippard, it would make him valuable to the historian of American culture. Along with Ned Buntline, George Foster, George Thompson, and several other sensationalists of the 1840s, Lippard brought to American literature a zestful new popular genre—the inexpensive serial novel—which, like the penny press it in part grew from, revolutionized the reportage of current events in American cities. Besides anticipating various future types of urban exposé fiction, the serial novel was the distant ancestor of the radio and television series, with a central cast of characters moving through a succession of adventurous plots in periodic installments that were discontinued when public interest began to run thin. Appearing either in cheap periodicals or as paper-covered volumes embellished with eye-catching melodramatic woodcuts, this fiction was peddled in railway stations and publishing-house book depots, forerunners of the bus stations, airports, supermarkets, and drug stores where today's readers buy diverting and quickly consumed paperbacks. A sociological reason for the popularity of such fiction was the increased mobility of Americans resulting from the railroad and the steamboat. As A. J. H. Duganne noted, Lippard's *The Quaker City* was "one of those works which are sure of a rapid sale wherever there is a migratory or floating population."[36] Fiction like Lippard's helped relieve the boredom of many a railway passage, just as fast-paced novels of sex and intrigue entertain subway commuters and air passengers today.

It is significant that readers of Lippard's time found special appeal in novels on the "mysteries" of American cities. Most historians agree that in the rapid expansion of the 1830s and 1840s, American city dwellers lost social knowledge and physical contact with each other for the first time.[37] The city was suddenly an overwhelming place, almost as mythical in grandeur and horror as the frontier, and the novelist who described dark urban mysteries verbalized this new estrangement and awe. The typical reader was interested not so much in bleak portraits of alienation and dehumanization like Melville's "Bartleby the Scrivener" as in fiction that explored the gloomy side of city life while lending some measure of order or meaning to a bewildering environment.

One way to resolve the complexities of urban living was to picture a pious orphan who bravely survived misfortune in the city by clinging to domestic values and hopeful religion. Especially attractive to female readers, the domestic novel was popularized by such novelists as Joseph Alden, Elizabeth Oakes Smith, Fanny Fern, Maria Cummins, and Susan Warner. Lippard's city novels represented a different brand of timely fiction, the urban exposé, which in its boldness and raciness catered particularly to the male audience. The reader of the exposé could momentarily bask in the illusion that the complicated problems of the city were being solved—secret vice was being laid bare, poverty and crime were being explained, guilt was being apportioned and sin punished. Most exposés advanced a reassuringly simple thesis—the corrupt and complacent rich victimize the poor—and helped to defuse anxieties over puzzling social inequities and capitalist exploitation by converting them into mass entertainment.

   The Quaker City was a pivotal and influential work in fictional treatments of the American city. To be sure, Lippard's was hardly the first American work that exposed urban horrors: Brockden Brown's *Arthur Mervyn* (1799), the anonymously written *Journey to Philadelphia* (1804) and *Laura* (1809), John Neal's *Keep Cool* (1817), Catherine Sedgwick's *Clarence* (1830), and Frederick Thomas's *Clinton Bradshaw* (1835) were among the some twenty-five American city novels that had been published before *The Quaker City*. Lippard's novel contributed to the genre a new penny-press liveliness and *roman-feuilleton* egalitarianism that had been absent from the earlier works. The relatively tame pre-1844 city novel gave way after *The Quaker City* to semipornographic exposés of aristocratic iniquity in dens of vice and low-life despair and depravity in poor sections of town. Among the some fifty "city mysteries" novels published between 1844 and 1860 were three obvious imitations of Lippard: *Mysteries of Philadelphia; or, Scenes of Real Life in the Quaker City* (1848), Henri Foster's *Ellen Grafton. The Den of Crime: A Romance of Secret Life in the Empire City* (1850), and Harmer S. Warden's *Black Rolf; or, the Red Witch of Wissahickon; . . . . A Tale of Secret Crimes and Hidden Mysteries of Quakerdom* (1856). Nearly all the exposés were written in a style that Lippard popularized and claimed to have originated, a style making use, in his words, of "short sentences, abrupt paragraphs, dramatic manner of description."[38]

In spite of its attraction for the masses and its influence on American city fiction, *The Quaker City* is quite different from other popular urban novels of the period. The novel has a metaphysical scope, psychological depth, and symbolic imaginativeness lacking in the merely sensational exposés of the day. Unlike the concretely described gambling hells and whorehouses in the typical exposé, Monk Hall is a mythical structure whose origins are wreathed in uncertainty: it was first owned by a bachelor who was "a libertine, a gourmand, an astrologer and a wizard," but no one is sure of its history.[39] Some say it had been a monastery, others a nunnery, others a factory, others a church, but most would say they "knew nothing about the old brick nuisance" (42). Similarly, "no one knew" anything about its overseer, Devil-Bug, though most agree he came from hell (42). Monk Hall and its keeper are thus ambiguous and inexplicable, closer in symbolic proportions to settings and characters in Melville's or Hawthorne's fiction than to those of the sensational exposé. Like the riverboat *Fidèle* in Melville's *The Confidence Man,* Monk Hall is a place of sham, deception, masks—a place where conventional religion and morality is powerless before amorality and the forces of darkness. Like the Puritan wilderness in Hawthorne's "Young Goodman Brown," it is a scene of nightly revel where outwardly pious folk are brought together in a communion of sin. Lippard's corrupt aristocrats do not merely drink, gamble, and copulate, as do George Foster's or Ned Buntline's. They strike false poses in an effort to subvert virtue, and they play subtle psychological and sexual games to dupe or terrorize their victims.

More complex than the average exposé, *The Quaker City* at the same time extensively parodies the sentimental-domestic novel. We have seen how Lippard's early newspaper satire on the sentimentalists reappeared in his warning authors of "Lollypopitude" to skip over the gloomy chapter on Devil-Bug in his cellar. Elsewhere in *The Quaker City* it appears in images from the do-

mestic novel—family, hearthside bliss, orphans, dreams of pastoral beauty—that Lippard ironically overturns. Monk Hall is
the hellish opposite of the home of domestic fiction, a place where
a father tries to rape his daughter under the pretense of consoling
her, where flickering firelight illumines wild scenes of bacchan-
alia, where marriage is a sham arrangement to facilitate seduction,
where brothers and sisters are violently separated. Devil-Bug,
whose real name, Abijah K. Jones, is a caricature of social respectability, is constantly referred to as a "father" overseeing his
"children." A walking parody of the kindly father of domestic
fiction, he boasts of "'our leetle family joys'" in Monk Hall and
ironically describes his stormy criminal past as follows: "'My
life's been a purty quiet one. . . . Not many incidents to tell;
passed my years in the comfortable retiracy o' domestic felicity,
as Parson Pyne would say!'" (183, 188). The irony deepens when
we learn that Devil-Bug is indeed a father to Mabel, the woman
who most closely approximates the heroine of domestic fiction
yet who is rescued from misfortune not by her own pious resolve
but by the intervention of Devil-Bug. Another perversion of
fatherhood is F. A. T. Pyne, Mabel's other "father," who has
incestuously approached her in the past and who does so again,
using drugs and sentimental persuasion. Pointed parody on domestic motherhood is visible in Lippard's portrayal of Mother
Nancy Perkins, the head procuress at Monk Hall, and Long-
haired Bess, who arranges the seduction of Mary Arlington.
Mother Nancy, the picture of a benign grandmother as she sits
quietly in her armchair, is described as "the respectable Lady
Abbess of Monk-hall, . . . a good, dear old body" (65). Her
advice to Long-haired Bess, "'You can act the lady when you
like,'" is carried out when Bess poses as a friendly older woman
to lure Mary into Monk Hall (67).

   The studied reversal of domestic fiction occurs most frequently
in evil characters' use of sentimental devices as instruments of
persuasion. Bess befriends Mary and inveigles her to sin by ap-
pealing to her emotions: "'I told her a long story of my sorrows;
how I had been engaged to be married, how my lover had died
of consumption but a month ago; that he was sich a nice young

man, with curly hair, and hazel eyes, and that I was in black for his death. I put peach fur over her eyes, by the whole hand's full, I tell you'" (68). Such mawkish stories continue to dupe the impressionable Mary after she enters Monk Hall. Indeed, Mary, the caricature of the love-struck heroine of sentimental fiction, falls prey as much to her own illusions of domestic and pastoral bliss as to Gus Lorrimer's mental or physical appeal. When the sly Gus offers to marry her and take her to "'a cottage, a quiet home . . . amid the green leaves of embowering trees,'" Mary exclaims: "'Oh, how like romance will be the plain reality of our life!'" (111). As she sits in Monk Hall reading a domestic play, Bulwer's *Claude Mellnotte,* she dreams of "'a home, quiet and peaceful, as that which this book describes'" (108). Gus promises her a home even more beatific than the one in the play, but his designs are hardly pure: "While enchaining the mind of the Maiden, with a story full of Romance, it was his intention to wake her animal nature into full action" (109). He continues to exploit domestic devices when he arranges the sham marriage with the aid of Long-haired Bess. The wedding ceremony, the standard culmination of growing togetherness and happiness in domestic novels, becomes in Lippard's ironic version a monstrous hoax designed to destroy rather than reward virtue. At the ceremony the venal editor Petriken impersonates a reassuring parson, Mutchins the gambler dresses as a kind old uncle, and Mother Nancy Perkins appears as a smiling grandmother. Taken in by this seemingly sanctified and friendly scene, Mary willingly marries Gus. When she later learns that she has been fooled, her pastoral myth is at last shattered: "A new world had broken upon her soul, not a world of green trees, silver streams and pleasant flowers, but a chaos of ashes, and mouldering flame. . . . She had sprung from the maiden into the woman, but a blight was on her soul forever" (124).

Lippard's attack on sentimental-domestic techniques reaches full symbolic expression in a scene in which Byrnewood Arlington, having failed in his efforts to rescue his sister Mary from her false bridegroom, is locked by Devil-Bug inside the Tower Room of Monk Hall. The way Devil-Bug has decorated and arranged the room makes it look like a comfortable scene from a domestic novel: "There were the untouched refreshments, the cold chicken and the bottle of wine, giving the place the air of a quiet supper-room, there were the false book-cases, indicating a resort for meditation and study, there was the cheerful furnace, its glowing flame flashing through the half-closed doors, speaking a pleasant tale of fireside comforts and joys" (103–104). Thinking that he has found momentary respite from his problems, Byrnewood enjoys some wine and asks God to help him save his sister. Meanwhile, Devil-Bug is watching the scene through a glass door, murmuring gleefully that the wine is drugged with opium and trying to attract Byrnewood's attention. When Byrnewood turns around and sees Devil-Bug, he starts running angrily toward the glass door but trips over a floor spike that makes a huge trap door spring open before him. Suddenly "half of the Chamber was changed into one black and yawning chasm, and the lamp standing on the table suddenly disappeared, leaving the place wrapt in thick darkness" (104). Byrnewood totters on the edge of the chasm, feels his legs give out, and then falls with a shriek as Devil-Bug yells, "'Down—down—*down*! Ah-ha! Three stories—down—down—down! I wonders how that 'ill work!'" (105). Lippard has planted a bomb of demonism and irrationality in a scene of domestic serenity and bliss. He takes a brother with a noble cause, the defense of a sister's virtue, and places him in a quintessentially homelike scene that turns out to be one more illusion in a domain of false appearances and one more insubstantial shell over a yawning abyss.

In addition to its prolonged satire on domestic sentimentalists, *The Quaker City* takes passing shots at the penny press and the nativist novel. Buzby Poodle, the editor of the *Daily Black Mail,* prowls through the book like a hungry beast gorging on the blood of its victims. Not only do we hear much about his scandalmongering, but we watch it trivialize and sensationalize the entire central action of the novel when Poodle prints the goings on in Monk Hall and has one of his lackeys shout through the streets: "'Hello! De 'Daily Brack Mail.' 'Wonderful abduction case—Miss Arlington missing!' Wonder whar de debbil de murders is?

'Shockin' Calamity—Death of Albert Livingstone, Esq., and his wife—burned alive.' . . . Dats somefin horrible—De High Golly!' " (469). Elsewhere, Lippard directly parodies a nativist work, Rosamond Culberton's *Rosamond* (1836), one of the most vicious of the many American anti-Catholic novels published during the 1830s and 1840s. Culbertson had carried anti-Catholicism to an extreme by exposing an alleged plot by a priest and his lover to capture young boys and throw them into a large meat grinder that produced sausages for public consumption. In Lippard's ironic variation on the story, the nativist Syllabub Scissors announces to F. A. T. Pyne's anti-Catholic congregation that a recent Protestant missionary group in Rome has been ground up in a "large manufactory for Bologna sausages" in Vatican City (224). Asking his hearers if they are willing "to be made into sausage," Scissors gets their consent and arranges another group trip to Rome to convert the Pope.

What is curious about the literary satire in *The Quaker City* is that Lippard freely borrows from the very genre he attacks: from the nativist novel he gets pimps and procuresses overseeing mass depravity in a conventlike structure with a basement where corpses are thrown; from the penny press and the urban exposé he derives the reportage of sensational events in the city; from the sentimental-domestic novel he borrows a benign religion of the heart aligned against sectarianism. Although this combined dismissal and acceptance of literary modes seems contradictory, it in fact reinforces Lippard's overall manipulative strategy of mocking and exploiting as he sees fit. Unlike many popular writers of his day, Lippard is not interested in reassuringly simple attitudes, either toward other literary genres or toward the various themes he explores. The reduction of virtue to an enigma that Lippard admired in Brockden Brown's *Ormond* is evident throughout *The Quaker City*. Monk Hall is a place where conventional morality proves inoperable, where heroic courage rapidly dissolves into terrified cowardice, where spiritual innocence does not insure physical safety. Lippard creates a relative world in which the reader is deprived not only of predictable chronology and plot sequence but also of characters he can admire, holistic moral or literary values he can grasp, and an author he can completely trust.

In contrast to other popular novels of the period—e.g., William Ware's *Julian* (1841), Susan Warner's *The Wide, Wide World* (1851), Maria Cummins's *The Lamplighter* (1854)—*The Quaker City* lacks a firm moral center. One of the attractions of *The Quaker City* for the twentieth-century reader is the fact that no character in the novel is flawless. Mabel, the closest approximation of an idealized heroine in the book, turns out to be a rather docile simpleton controlled by outside forces, most of which are evil. The fact that she, the novel's most virtuous character, is the child of Devil-Bug, its most depraved figure, and that she survives only with his help, shows Lippard's ironic mixture of good and evil. This mixture is equally apparent in the other main characters: Dora Livingstone, a woman of admirable intellect and rich feelings who nevertheless is duped by her paramour's promise of wealth and a title; Dora's husband Albert, the wronged cuckold who understandably wreaks revenge on his wife but in the process becomes a savage murderer; Mary Arlington, whose innocent illusions prove to be her downfall; her brother Byrnewood, whose filial affection borders on incestuous devotion and whose vindictiveness runs over into sadism; Luke Harvey, who is driven to perform heroic deeds not by inner virtue but by envy and resentment; and Ravoni, the brilliant founder of a new humanitarian religion who runs to fanatical excess. The mixture is epitomized in Devil-Bug and Long-haired Bess, the monsters who become redemptive saviors. Lippard's fundamentally paradoxical view of human nature is encapsulated in his explanation of "the mass of contradictions" in Bess's character:

One moment conversing in the slang of a brothel, like a thing lapped from birth in pollution; the next, whispering forth her ravings in language indicative of the educated woman of her purer days; one instant glorifying in her shame, the next recoiling in horror as she viewed the dark path which she had trodden, the darker path which she was yet to tread—these paradoxes are things of every day occurrence, only to be explained, when the mass of good and evil, found in every human heart, is divided into distinct parts, no more to mingle in one, no more to occasion an eternal contest in the self-warring heart of man. (71)

The Quaker City is a challenging and disturbing book, one that seems to have been written, to use Mark Twain's phrase, with a pen warmed up in hell. Lippard's attack on Philadelphia aristocrats is hardly the most frightening feature of the novel; if it were, the book would be just one more simple formulaic social statement characteristic of the popular urban-exposé school of the 1840s. Far more thought-provoking are resonant tensions and conflicts that Lippard intentionally leaves unresolved: innocence versus monstrosity, sanity versus irrationality, purity versus animality, illusion versus reality, hopeful religion versus visions of nothingness. Perhaps the final irony about the book is that it was very popular. Clearly the mass of readers fastened on the entertaining features of the novel—the colorful characters with funny names, the heaving bosoms, the madcap adventure—without recognizing the problematic metaphysics below the racy surface. Lippard's special achievement was producing a book that forcefully challenged convention yet that managed to regale the masses.

Surveying Lippard's literary career, we find evidence of his connections with major American literature other than the exploration of conflicts and paradoxes in *The Quaker City*. For instance, Lippard's descriptions of the Wissahickon countryside in his Revolutionary legends were powerful enough to induce the seventeen-year-old Mark Twain to write in 1853: "Geo. Lippard in his *Legends of Washington and His Generals* has rendered the Wissahickon sacred in my eyes, and I shall make that trip, as well as one to Germantown, soon."[40] If Mark Twain appreciated the nature passages in *Washington and His Generals,* he probably also enjoyed scenes of vernacular comedy in the book, especially one involving a crusty patriot who talks in back-country dialect to a laughably incognizant Hessian soldier he has taken prisoner. We do not know whether Mark Twain read any of Lippard's other works, but if he had, he would have discovered that Lippard regularly created characters—Rumpus Grizzle of "The Spermaceti Papers," Devil-Bug of *The Quaker City,* Jacob Mayland and

the Oath-Bound Five of *Blanche of Brandywine,* John Hoffman of
The Empire City—who are used as vernacular vehicles against
pretense and elitism in a way that anticipates Mark Twain's lowly
personae.

Recent scholars have noticed that Lippard can be connected
with other familiar authors as well. Emilio de Grazia finds certain
of Lippard's wizard figures and overreaching monomaniacs similar
to characters in Melville and Hawthorne.[41] Heyward Ehrlich
places Lippard's apocalyptic religious imagery in the cosmological
sermon tradition of Michael Wigglesworth and Jonathan Edwards; after comparing Lippard to a few established writers of
the American Renaissance, Ehrlich goes on to call his city novels
prophetic of Stephen Crane, Frank Norris, Theodore Dreiser,
Jack London, John Dos Passos, and Norman Mailer.[42] Leslie
Fiedler also links Lippard with London and Mailer and argues
that Mailer's *An American Dream* is "closer to what Lippard was
doing in *The Quaker City* than anything written in between."[43]

Lippard could indeed be compared to these authors and more,
with qualifications and explanations in each case. There has been
a recent tendency, however, to overcompensate for Lippard's longtime obscurity by searching for respectable analogues to him in
an effort to prop him up, with the reputations of better-known
writers being used as support. Although valuable in the historical
placement of Lippard, such comparisons ignore the fact that he
is a complex writer whose life and works merit close scrutiny on
their own, without artificial references to more established authors. In a sense, Lippard has become the victim of his popularity.
Not only have most of the original editions of his paper-covered
novels crumbled into dust, but also he has been subject to a
condescension that has appeared variously as outright neglect,
apologetic defense, or frenetic listings of familiar writers to whom
he can be compared. The time has come for renewed study of
Lippard on the part of those interested in antebellum literature
and society. Lippard was an unusual combination of the popular
writer and the exploratory genius, with one foot planted in as-

cendant mass culture, the other in the major literature of the American Renaissance, and with an eye peering into a future that would forget him all too soon.

Notes and References

Chapter One

1. Edwin C. Jellett Ms., 1902, Germantown Historical Society.

2. "The Destroyer of the Homestead" (1849), in the *White Banner,* ed. George Lippard, 1 (Philadelphia, 1851):107.

3. Charles Chauncey Burr, Introductory Essay to George Lippard, *Washington and His Generals; or, Legends of the Revolution* (Philadelphia, 1847), p. iv.

4. [John Bell Bouton], *The Life and Choice Writings of George Lippard* (New York, 1855), p. 15.

5. James B. Elliott, "Biographical Sketch of George Lippard," introduction to Lippard, *Thomas Paine, Author-Soldier of the American Revolution* (Philadelphia, 1894), p. 15.

6. This newspaper, which DuSolle founded in 1837 and edited until 1849, is not to be confused with W. T. Porter's famous New York journal *Spirit of the Times* (1831–1861).

7. *Spirit of the Times,* February 7 and February 10, 1842.

8. Lippard, *Herbert Tracy, or The Legend of the Black Rangers* (Philadelphia, 1844), p. vi.

9. *Citizen Soldier,* November 15, 1843.

10. In Lippard, *Herbert Tracy,* pp. 166–67.

11. Lippard to Robert Morris, August 3, 1844, Historical Society of Pennsylvania.

12. Lippard to Morris.

13. [Bouton], p. 19.

14. *Philadelphia Public Ledger,* November 5, 1844.

15. Francis C. Wemyss, *Twenty-Six Years of the Life of an Actor and Manager* (New York, 1847), p. 19.

16. [Bouton], p. 19.

17. Wemyss, p. 398.

18. Quoted in Joseph Jackson, "George Lippard: Poet of the Proletariat" (ca. 1930), unpublished manuscript in Historical Society of Pennsylvania, Chapter 8, p. 31.

19. *Massachusetts Quarterly* 1 (December 1847):125.

20. *New Monthly Magazine* 74 (1845):238.

21. *Spirit of the Times,* January 17, 1845.

22. Quoted in Joseph Jackson, "A Bibliography of the Works of George Lippard," *Pennsylvania Magazine of History and Biography* 54 (April 1930):134.

23. Lippard, *The Quaker City; or, The Monks of Monk Hall* (1844–1845; rpt. Philadelphia, 1876), Preface, p. (1).

24. Duganne, *The Knights of the Seal; or, The Mysteries of the Three Cities* (Philadelphia: Colon and Andriance, 1845), p. 26.

25. *Saturday Courier,* July 4, 1846.

26. Ibid., December 26, 1846.

27. Philadelphia's *United States Saturday Post,* September 25, 1846.

28. *Saturday Courier,* May 29, 1847.

29. *John-Donkey,* January 1, 1848. One of the three editors of this weekly was Thomas Dunn English, whom Lippard had satirized as "Thomas Done Brown" in "The Bread Crust Papers" (1842).

30. Motley Manners (pseudonym of A. J. H. Duganne), *Holden's Dollar Magazine* 2 (July 1848):422, 423.

31. This letter and other correspondence between Lippard and Taylor appeared in the *Washington Union,* May 26, 1849.

32. *Quaker City* weekly, June 23, 1849.

33. *Quaker City* weekly, May 12, 1849.

34. *Quaker City* weekly, January 26, 1850.

35. Quoted in Arthur Hobson Quinn, *Edgar Allan Poe: A Critical Biography* (New York: D. Appleton-Century, 1941), p. 621.

36. *Quaker City* weekly, October 28, 1849. Quotations from this periodical in the first two paragraphs of Section III are cited parenthetically in the text, with the abbreviation *QCW* used to designate the paper's title.

37. The Brotherhood of the Union, "Notes on the First Annual Convocation" (October 1850), microfilmed manuscript in Historical Society of Pennsylvania.

38. Roger Butterfield, "George Lippard and His Secret Brotherhood," *Pennsylvania Magazine of History & Biography,* 74 (July 1955):298.

39. Lippard to George Baker, August 10, 1852, manuscript in Historical Society of Pennsylvania.

40. Lippard, "Notes on the Brotherhood of the Union" (Philadelphia, ca 1852), pp. 3–4, manuscript in Historical Society of Pennsylvania. Hereafter cited parenthetically in the text as "Brotherhood Notes." A 72-page abridgment of *The B. G. C.*—the only copy known—is in the library of the American Antiquarian Society.

41. [Bouton], p. 128.
42. This is Bouton's paraphrase of Lippard's toast in *Life and Choice Writings,* pp. 94–95.
43. P. R. Gardner (?) to Lippard, December 5, 1853, manuscript in Historical Society of Pennsylvania.
44. [Bouton], p. 121.
45. Sarah Lippard Bilbough, "A Leaf from Grandfather's Bible," p. 12, microfilmed manuscript in Historical Society of Pennsylvania.
46. *Philadelphia Public Ledger,* February 10, 1854.
47. *Philadelphia Sunday Mercury,* March 5, 1854.
48. *Camden Post-Telegram,* April 15, 1822.
49. "Brotherhood Notes," p. 7.

Chapter Two

1. See Margaret Dalzeil, *Popular Fiction 100 Years Ago* (London: Cohen and West, 1957), pp. 15–16.
2. See Nora Atkinson, *Eugène Sue et Le Roman-Feuilleton* (Paris: A. Nizet and M. Bastard, 1929), Chapter 1.
3. For a general description of Sand's fiction, see the Introduction to Patricia Thompson, *George Sand and the Victorians* (New York: Columbia University Press, 1977).
4. *Philadelphia Public Ledger,* October 5, 1844.
5. See, for example, Lippard's praise of Sue in the *Quaker City* weekly, December 30, 1848, and in *The White Banner* 1 (Philadelphia, 1851):152.
6. Frank Luther Mott, *American Journalism, a History: 1690–1960,* Third Edition (New York: Macmillan, 1962), Chapter 13.
7. George Foster, *Fifteen Minutes Around New York* (New York: Dewitt and Davenport, 1854), p. 24.
8. *Citizen Soldier,* June 28, 1843, and *Saturday Courier,* August 29, 1846.
9. *The Nazarene; or, The Last of the Washingtons* (Philadelphia, 1846), p. 123.
10. John Neal, *Seventy-Six; or, Love and Battle* (1822; rpt., London: J. Cunningham, 1840), p. 69.
11. *The Quaker City,* pp. 1–2.
12. David Brion Davis, *Homicide in American Fiction, 1798–1860: A Study in Social Values* (Ithaca, N.Y.: Cornell University Press, 1957), p. 206.

13. *Quaker City* weekly, December 30, 1848, and *The Empire City; or, New York by Night and Day* (1849; rpt., Philadelphia, 1864), p. 90.

14. *'Bel of Prairie Eden. A Romance of Mexico* (Boston, 1848), pp. 58–59.

15. George Thompson, *City Crimes; or, Life in New York and Boston* (Boston: William Berry & Co., 1849), p. 31.

16. Anon., *Revelations of Asmodeus; or, Mysteries of Upper Ten-Dom* (New York: C. G. Graham & Co., 1849), p. 38.

17. *The Quaker City*, p. 272.

18. *The Ladye Annabel*, reprinted as *The Mysteries of Florence* (Philadelphia, 1864), p. 56.

19. *Washington and His Generals*, reprinted as *The Legends of the American Revolution. "1776." Or, Washington and His Generals* (Philadelphia, 1876), p. 72.

20. *Blanche of Brandywine; or, September the Eighth to Eleventh, 1777* (1846; rpt., Philadelphia, 1876), p. 223.

21. The early surrealists were not aware of Lippard, but praised several novelists who influenced him, including Ann Radcliffe, "Monk" Lewis, and Edgar Allan Poe. See J. H. Matthews, *Surrealism and the Novel* (Ann Arbor: University of Michigan Press, 1966), Chapter 1, and André Breton, *What Is Surrealism? Selected Writings,* ed. Franklin Rosemont (London: Pluto Press, 1978), pp. 84–85, 372.

22. Thompson Westcott, "Philadelphia and the Philadelphians in 1850," *Philadelphia Sunday Dispatch,* October 13, 1850.

23. *Spirit of the Times,* February 19, 1842.

24. *Citizen Soldier,* June 14, 1843.

25. *Blanche of Brandywine,* pp. 215, 199.

26. *The Quaker City,* p. 91.

27. Breton p. 122, and Hugnet, quoted in J. H. Matthews, *An Introduction to Surrealism* (University Park: Pennsylvania State University Press, 1965), p. 64.

28. *The Quaker City,* pp. 21, 42.

29. *The Midnight Queen; or, Leaves from New-York Life* (New York, 1853), p. 78.

30. Introductory Essay to Lippard, *Washington and His Generals: or, Legends of the Revolution* (Philadelphia, 1847), p. xiv.

31. Jean-Louis Bory, *Eugène Sue: Le Roi Du Roman Populaire* (Paris: Hachette, 1962), p. 127.

32. *Paul Ardenheim; The Monk of Wissahikon. A Romance of the American Revolution. "1776."* (1848; rpt. Philadelphia, 1876), pp. 533–34.

33. *The Nazarene,* p. vii.

34. See Alex de Jonge, *Nightmare Culture. Lautréamont and "Les Chants de Maldoror"* (London: Secker and Warburg, 1973), pp. 51–68, 84–91.

35. *The Empire City,* p. 46.

36. *Quaker City* weekly, May 12, 1849.

Chapter Three

1. *The Man with the Mask; A Sequel to Memoirs of a Preacher* (Philadelphia, 1849), p. 25.

2. *New York: Its Upper Ten and Lower Million* (Cincinnati, 1853), p. 317.

3. *The Memoirs of a Preacher* (1849; rpt. Phila., 1864), p. 9.

4. *New York,* p. 139.

5. Ibid., p. 229.

6. "Jesus and the Poor," *Nineteenth Century* 1 (1848):71.

7. *Memoirs of a Preacher,* p. 35.

8. *The Quaker City,* p. 343.

9. *Memoirs of a Preacher,* p. 41.

10. *New York,* p. 199.

11. *The Nazarene,* p. 94.

12. *The Empire City,* p. 86.

13. Ibid., p. 173.

14. *Memoirs of a Preacher,* pp. 19–20.

15. See Umberto Eco, "Rhetoric and Ideology in Sue's *Les Mystères de Paris," International Social Science Journal* 19 (1967):551–69.

16. *Spirit of the Times,* March 3, 1842.

17. *Quaker City* weekly, February 10, 1849.

18. "George Lippard: Poet of the Proletariat," unpublished manuscript in the Joseph Jackson Collection, Historical Society of Pennsylvania, ca. 1930.

19. See Bory, pp. 245–48.

20. Eco, p. 566.

21. *Midnight Queen,* p. 72.

22. *Memoirs of a Preacher,* p. 35.

23. *The Nazarene,* pp. 138–39.

24. *Adonai: The Pilgrim of Eternity,* in *White Banner* 1 (1851):59.

25. *The Empire City,* p. 51.

26. R. Swinburne Clymer, *The Book of Rosicruciae* (Quakertown, Pa.: Philosophical Publishing Co., 1947), p. 136.

27. *Herbert Tracy,* p. 35.

28. *The Quaker City,* p. 328.

29. *The Nazarene,* p. 120.

30. *The Man with the Mask,* p. 33.

31. *Quaker City* weekly, February 9, 1850.

32. *Legends of the American Revolution,* p. 272.

33. *Midnight Queen,* p. 104.

34. *Quaker City* weekly, June 2, 1849.

35. "The Monster with Three Names" (1849), reprinted in *The White Banner,* pp. 113–16.

36. *Adonai,* in *The White Banner,* p. 96.

37. See Henry J. Ford, "The Liberty Bell, " *American Mercury* 3 (November 1924):279–84. Lippard's legend was unrelated to myths about the cracking of the Liberty Bell, which in reality occurred in 1831 when the bell was rung for the death of John Randolph.

38. *Saturday Courier,* January 2, 1847.

39. *United States Saturday Post,* September 25, 1846, and New York's *Holden's Dollar Magazine* 2 (July 1848):424.

40. *Sunday Dispatch,* November 3, 1850.

41. *Legends of Mexico; or, The Battles of Old Rough and Ready* (1847; rpt. London, 1849), p. 57.

42. There is no evidence, however, to support R. Swinburne Clymer's claim that Lippard joined a Philadelphia order of Rosicrucians in the mid-1840s (see *The Book of Rosicruciae,* pp. 138–39).

43. Elliott, "Biographical Sketch of George Lippard," pp. 4–5.

44. *Legends of the American Revolution,* pp. 522, 270.

45. *Blanche of Brandywine,* p. 162.

46. *Legends of the American Revolution,* p. 107.

47. *Legends of Mexico,* pp. 20, 137–38.

48. Ibid., p. 56.

49. Ibid. and *Legends of the American Revolution,* p. 526.

50. *Legends of the American Revolution,* p. 525.

51. *Philadelphia Press Magazine,* September 16, 1917.

52. *Philadelphia Evening Public Ledger,* November 2, 1939.

Chapter Four

1. *Life and Choice Writings,* pp. 90, 45.

2. For an account of early satirical and affirmative religious fiction in America, and its influence on Lippard's writings, see David S. Rey-

nolds, *Faith in Fiction: The Emergence of Religious Literature in America* (Cambridge, Mass.: Harvard University Press, 1981).

3. "Can You Tell Me Why Protestantism is a Failure?" in *The White Banner*, p. 136.

4. *Quaker City* weekly, December 30, 1848.

5. *The Ladye Annabel*, pp. 145, 147.

6. *Paul Ardenheim*, p. 302.

7. *The Quaker City*, p. 48.

8. *The Nazarene*, p. 59.

9. *New York*, p. 69.

10. *The Empire City*, p. 90.

11. *Memoirs of a Preacher*, p. 12.

12. *New York*, pp. 113–14.

13. *The Quaker City*, p. 170.

14. New York's *Holden's Dollar Magazine* 2 (July 1848):423.

15. *The Quaker City*, p. 228.

16. *Memoirs of a Preacher*, p. 211.

17. "Religion," in *The White Banner*, p. 120.

18. *Philadelphia Sunday Dispatch*, October 27, 1850.

19. *New York*. p. 70.

20. *Legends of the American Revolution*, p. 405.

21. *Sunday Dispatch*, November 3, 1850.

22. *Paul Ardenheim*, p. 61.

23. "The Heart-Broken," in *Nineteenth Century* 1 (1848):25, and *New York*, p. 231.

24. *Adonai*, in *The White Banner*, pp. 69–70.

25. *Life and Choice Writings*, p. 84.

26. The message bears the date "January 20" without designating a year. Manuscript in the archives of the Historical Society of Pennsylvania.

27. *The Man with the Mask*, p. 67.

28. *Quaker City* weekly, May 12, 1849.

29. *Legends of the American Revolution*, p. 309.

30. *Citizen Soldier*, August 2, 1843.

31. *Quaker City* weekly, May 19, 1849.

32. Ibid., December 30, 1848.

33. "The Heart-Broken," p. 22.

34. *Memoirs of a Preacher*, p. 59.

35. *The White Banner*, p. 137.

36. *The Quaker City*, p. 21.

37. *Memoirs of a Preacher*, p. 82.

38. Charles Chauncey Burr, review of *The Nazarene,* in *Nineteenth Century* 1 (1848):360.

39. *New York,* p. 114.

40. *Sunday Dispatch,* November 3, 1850.

41. *Legends of the American Revolution,* pp. 442, 444.

42. *The Quaker City,* p. 228.

43. *Quaker City* weekly, August 11, 1849.

44. See Fred Allen Briggs, "Didactic Literature in America, 1825–1850," Ph.D. Dissertation, Indiana University, 1954.

Chapter Five

1. *Philadelphia Daily Chronicle,* August 17, 1844.

2. See Ann Douglas, *The Feminization of American Culture* (New York: Knopf, 1977), and George B. Forgie, *Patricide in the House Divided: A Psychological Interpretation of Lincoln and His Age* (New York: Norton, 1979).

3. *Spirit of the Times,* March 28, 1842.

4. *Citizen Soldier,* June 21, 1843.

5. *Citizen Soldier,* July 7 and July 5, 1843. Quotations from the *Citizen Soldier* in the remainder of this paragraph are cited parenthetically in the text, with the abbreviation *CS* used to designate the periodical's title.

6. *The Quaker City,* pp. 258–59.

7. *Spirit of the Times,* February 7, 1842. The other quotation from the *Spirit of the Times* in this paragraph is cited parenthetically in the text, with the abbreviation *ST* used to designate the periodical's title.

8. *Quaker City* weekly, March 17, 1849.

9. *Citizen Soldier,* October 10, 1843.

10. *Nineteenth Century* 1 (1848):21, 22, 23.

11. Lippard to Cooper, August 3, 1844, manuscript in the Yale Cooper Papers.

12. *Quaker City* weekly, April 21, 1849. Quotations from the *Quaker City* weekly in this and the following two paragraphs are cited parenthetically in the text, with *QCW* used to designate the periodical's title.

13. *Quaker City* weekly, December 30, 1848 and *Adonai,* in *The White Banner,* p. 37.

14. *The White Banner,* p. 148.

15. *Quaker City* weekly, February 10, 1849.

16. *Citizen Soldier,* July 5, 1843.

17. *'Bel of Prairie Eden,* p. 73.

18. *Blanche of Brandywine,* p. 339.

19. *Massachusetts Quarterly* 1 (December 1847):125.

20. *Philadelphia Sunday Dispatch,* September 22 and October 6, 1850.

21. *Philadelphia Sunday Times,* August 1, 1886.

22. Inscription in Poe, *Eureka: A Prose Poem* (New York: G. P. Putnam, 1848), manuscript in the Free Library, Philadelphia.

23. *Quaker City* weekly, October 28, 1849.

24. *Citizen Soldier,* November 28, 1843.

25. *Quaker City* weekly, June 2, 1849.

26. Ellis P. Oberholtzer, *The Literary History of Philadelphia* (Philadelphia: G. W. Jacobs and Co., 1906), pp. 257–58.

27. *Quaker City* weekly, May 12, 1849.

28. *Herbert Tracy,* p. 167.

29. *Sunday Dispatch,* October 6, 1850.

30. Introductory essay to *Washington and His Generals,* p. xxiv.

31. *Marginalia,* in *The Works of Edgar Allan Poe* (Chicago: Stone and Kimball, 1895), 7:259–60.

32. New York's *Holden's Dollar Magazine* 2 (July 1848):423.

33. D. H. Lawrence, *Studies in Classic American Literature* (1923; rpt. New York: Viking, 1968), p. 81.

34. *Mysteries of Florence,* p. 246.

35. Bennett Book Studio advertisement for *The Rose of Wissahikon* (New York, 1943), Historical Society of Pennsylvania.

36. *Holden's Dollar Magazine* 2 (July 1848):423.

37. Michael Feldberg, *The Philadelphia Riots of 1844: A Study of Ethnic Conflict* (Westport, Conn.: Greenwood Press, 1975), p. 12.

38. *Philadelphia Saturday Courier,* July 12, 1847.

39. *The Quaker City,* p. 41.

40. Samuel Langhorne Clemens to his brother Orion, October 26, 1853, in Albert B. Paine, *Mark Twain. A Biography* (New York: Harper, 1912), 1:100. Mark Twain was then a printer on the *Philadelphia Inquirer.*

41. Emilio de Grazia, "The Life and Works of George Lippard," Ph.D. Dissertation, Ohio State University, 1969.

42. Heyward Ehrlich, "The 'Mysteries' of Philadelphia: Lippard's *Quaker City* and 'Urban' Gothic," *ESQ: A Journal of the American Renaissance* 18 (1st Quarter 1972):50–65.

43. Leslie Fiedler, "The Male Novel," *Partisan Review* 37 (1970):76.

Selected Bibliography

PRIMARY SOURCES

1. Separately Published Works by George Lippard

This list contains Lippard's writings that appeared either in bound or pamphlet form. Where no copy of a volume has been located, the title is given in brackets. In cases where a work had been previously published in a periodical, the date and place of the initial publication is mentioned.

[*Adrian, the Neophyte*. Philadelphia: I. R. and A. H. Diller, 1843.]
    First published in the *Philadelphia Citizen Soldier*, 1843.

"The B. G. C." [exact title unknown]. Secret ritual and degree work of the Brotherhood of the Union. Lippard called this the B. G. C., and said it was a work of two hundred pages. No such copy is known, but an abridged version of seventy-two pages, with cover title "B. G. C.," is at the American Antiquarian Society in Worcester, Massachusetts.

The Battle-Day of Germantown. Philadelphia: A. H. Diller, 1843. First published in the *Citizen Soldier*, 1843.

Blanche of Brandywine; or, September the Eleventh, 1777. A Romance, Combining the Poetry, Legend, and History of the Battle of Brandywine. Philadelphia: G. B. Zieber & Co., 1846. Two "1846" reprintings by T. B. Peterson, who also printed an edition in 1876. Translation: Adolf Strodtmann, *Blanche von Brandywine; oder, Der efte September 1777*. Hamburg: Verlags-Comptoir, 1859. Recent edition: *Blanche of Brandywine*. Freeport, N.Y.: Books for Libraries Press, 1969.

'Bel of Prairie Eden. A Romance of Mexico. Philadelphia: T. B. Peterson, 1848. First published serially in the Boston weekly *Uncle Sam*, 1848. Reprinted ca. 1870 as Number 58 in DeWitt's Ten Cent Romance Series.

The Brotherhood of the Rosy Cross: The First World Parliament and Meeting of the Council of Seven, The Consecration of Washington the Deliverer, Fulfillment of the Prophecy [seventy-five pages of alledgedly Rosi crucian material selected from Lippard's *Paul Ardenheim* and *Legends of the American Revolution*]. Quakertown, Penn.: Rosicrucian Foundation, 1935. Introduction by R. Swinburne Clymer.

The Empire City; or, New York by Night and Day. New York: Stringer and Townsend, 1850. Early installments published serially in the *Quaker City* weekly, 1849. Reprinted in 1864 by the Petersons. Translation: *Die Empire City, oder New-York bei Nacht und Tag.* New York: F. Rauchfuss, 1854, and Hamburg: Verlags-Comptoir, 1859. Recent edition: *The Empire City.* Freeport, N.Y.: Books for Libraries Press, 1969.

The Entranced; or, the Wanderer of Eighteen Centuries. Philadelphia: Joseph Severns and Co, n.d. [1849]. First ran serially in the *Quaker City* weekly in 1849. Was revised and reprinted as *Adonai: The Pilgrim of Eternity* in *The White Banner* (Philadelphia: George Lippard, 1851).

The Heart-Broken [tribute to Charles Brockden Brown]. Philadelphia: G. B. Zieber & Co., 1848. First published in the *Philadelphia Nineteenth Century,* 1848.

Herbert Tracy, or The Legend of the Black Rangers. Philadelphia: R. G. Berford, 1844. First published serially in Philadelphia's *United States Saturday Post,* 1842.

The Killers. A Narrative of Real Life in Philadelphia . . . By a Member of the Philadelphia Bar. Philadelphia: Hankinson and Bartholomew, 1850. First printed serially in the *Quaker City* weekly, 1849. Reissued as *The Bank Director's Son, A Real and Intensely Interesting Revelation of City Life. . . .* Philadelphia: E. E. Barclay, 1851.

The Ladye Annabel; or, The Doom of the Poisoner. A Romance by an Unknown Author. Philadelphia: R. G. Berford, 1844. First published serially in the *Citizen Soldier,* 1843–1844. Reprinted in 1845 by G. B. Zieber. Later reissued under the following titles: *The Ladye Annabel: A Romance of the Alembic, the Altar, and the Throne.* Philadelphia: G. B. Zieber and Co., 1849; *Ladye Annabel, or The Child of Aldarin.* Philadelphia: T. B. Peterson & Brothers, 1854; *The Mysteries of Florence.* Philadelphia: T. B. Peterson & Brothers, 1864.

Legends of Mexico. Philadelphia: T. B. Peterson, 1847. Later Peterson editions appeared in 1849, 185–?, and 1876. Reprinted as *Legends of Mexico; or, The Battles of Old Rough and Ready.* London: J. S. Pratt, 1849.

The Man with the Mask; A Sequel to The Memoirs of a Preacher, a Revelation of the Church and the Home. Philadelphia: Joseph Severns and Company, n.d. [1849]. First published serially in the *Quaker City*

weekly, 1849. Gathered together with *Memoirs of a Preacher* and
published in 1864 by the Petersons as *Memoirs of a Preacher; or,
Mysteries of the Pulpit.*

[*The* Memoirs of a Preacher, a Revelation of the Church and the Home.
Philadelphia: Joseph Severns and Company, 1849.] First printed
serially in the *Quaker City* weekly, beginning December 30, 1848.
Reprinted as *Mysteries of the Pulpit; or, a Revelation of the Church
and the Home.* Philadelphia: E. E. Barclay, 1851 and 1852. Gathered together with *The Man with the Mask* and published by the
Petersons in 1864 as *Memoirs of a Preacher; or, Mysteries of the Pulpit.*

The Midnight Queen; or, Leaves from New-York Life. New York: Garrett
& Co., 1853. Contains three stories: "The Midnight Queen," "The
Life of a Man of the World," and "Margaret Dunbar," Reissued
by Dick & Fitzgerald, New York, n.d. [not before 1858].

*The Nazarene; or, The Last of the Washingtons. A Revelation of Philadelphia,
New York and Washington in the Year 1844.* Philadelphia: G. Lippard and Co., 1846. Three of the projected twenty-four parts
published by Lippard's company, which went bankrupt. Parts Four
and Five published the same year by John A. Bell and G. B.
Zieber, respectively. The Petersons reissued the book in 1854.

New York: Its Upper Ten and Lower Million. Cincinnati: H. M. Rulison,
1853. Reprinted by Rulison in 1854; separate 1854 edition published in Cincinnati by E. Mendenhall. Czech-Bohemian Translation: *Tajnosti New Yorkse* (New York: Dělnické Listy, ca. 1890).
Recent edition: *New York: Its Upper Ten and Lower Million.* Upper
Saddle River, N.J.: Literature House, 1970.

Paul Ardenheim, The Monk of Wissahikon. Philadelphia: T. B. Peterson,
1848. Reprinted by Peterson in 1876 as *Paul Ardenheim; The Monk
of Wissahikon. A Romance of the American Revolution.* "1776."

*The Quaker City; or, The Monks of Monk Hall. A Romance of Philadelphia
Life, Mystery and Crime.* [Anon.] Philadelphia: G. B. Zieber &
Co., 1844. Issued in ten paper-covered parts, four of which appeared in 1844, the remainder in 1845. All parts collected and
published as a single volume in May 1845. "Sixteenth edition"
published "by the author" in 1846. "Twenty-seventh American
edition" published in 1849 by T. B. Peterson under the title *The
Quaker City. A Romance of the Rich and Poor.* Reprinted in 1876
under original title by T. B. Peterson and Brothers and by Leary,
Stuart & Co., Philadelphia. Pirated editions: Friedrich Gerstäcker,
Die Quakerstadt und ihre Geheimnisse. Leipsig: Otto Wigland, 1846;
Dora Livingstone, the Adulteress; or, The Quaker City. London: G.

Purkess, [1848]. Recent editions: *The Monks of Monk Hall*. Introduction by Leslie Fiedler. New York: Odyssey Press, 1970; *Die Quakerstadt und ihre Geheimnisse*. Munich: C. Hanser, ca. 1971.

The Rose of Wissahikon; or, The Fourth of July, 1776. A Romance, Embracing the Secret History of the Declaration of Independence. Philadelphia: G. B. Zieber & Co., 1847. First printed in the *Philadelphia Semi-Annual Pictorial Saturday Courier*, 1847.

Thomas Paine, Author-Soldier of the American Revolution. Philadelphia: n.p., ca. 1894. Edited with a biographical introduction by James B. Elliott. A lecture Lippard gave at least three times (first on January 26, 1846).

Washington and His Generals; or, Legends of the Revolution . . . With a Biographical Sketch of the Author, by Rev. C. Chauncey Burr. Philadelphia: G. B. Zieber & Co., 1847. Two editions printed in "1847" by T. B. Peterson, who reissued the work in 1876 as *The Legends of the American Revolution. "1776." Or, Washington and His Generals*. Translation: *Legenden aus americanischen Revolution*. Philadelphia: F. W. Thomas, 1857. Recent edition: *Washington and His Generals; or, Legends of the Revolution*. Freeport, N.Y.: Books for Libraries Press, 1971.

Washington and His Men. Philadelphia: Jos. Severns and Company, 1849. Reprinted as *Washington and His Men: A New Series of Legends of the Revolution*. New York: Stringer & Townsend, 1850; *Washington and His Men. Being the "Second Series" of the Legends of the American Revolution "1776."* Philadelphia: T. B. Peterson & Bros., 1864.

The White Banner. Vol. I. Philadelphia: George Lippard: Publisher, on Behalf of the Shareholders, 1851.

2. Chronological List of Lippard's Periodical Publications

Space does not permit a complete list of the stories, essays, literary criticism, and news reports that Lippard published in periodicals. The following list is a sampling of representative or significant works other than the serialized fiction mentioned above.

A. *Spirit of the Times* (Philadelphia daily newspaper edited by John S. DuSolle). All Lippard entries in the 1842 issue.

"City Police" column by "Billy Brier"—Early January through April 8. "Our Talisman" series—January 11 through February 17.

"Letter" [by Lippard] from Charles Dickens to "William Brier, Esq."—March 8.

"Boz in Philadelphia"—March 9.

"The Sanguine Poetaster. A Tale by Eric Iterbil"—March 22.

"The Bread Crust Papers—The Duel in Camden"—March 28 through April 1.

"The Wickedest Thing Alive *(An Apologue from the Arabian MSS).* By A. Brownson Smallcut"—April 9.

B. *Citizen Soldier: A Weekly Newspaper, Devoted to the Interests of the Volunteers and Militia of the United States* (Philadelphia newspaper edited by Isaac R. and Adam H. Diller).

"Legend of the Midnight Death, a Story of the Wissahikon"—January 19, 1843.

"The Spermaceti Papers. By Geoffrey"—May 31 through August 26, 1843.

"The Legend of the Coffee Bags"—:June 7, 1843.

"American Literature"—June 21, 1843.

"The Men of the Revolution"—August 16 and 24 and October 4, 1843.

"The Walnut Coffin Papers . . . The Uprisings of the Coffin-Maker's 'Prentice"—September 20 and October 11, 1843.

Article praising war—October 11, 1843.

Review of Edgar Allan Poe's "Lecture on American Poetry"—November 15, 1843.

Comment on Poe's departure from *Graham's*—November 29, 1843.

[Same, retitled *Home Journal and Citizen Soldier.*]

Call for a magazine edited by Poe—January 10, 1844.

"Jesus the Democrat"—January 31, 1844.

"The King of the Spirit Band"—February 14, 1844.

"The Buck-Shot War, or Philadelphia . . . in the Winter of '38 and '39"—April 3, 1844, and weekly for at least a month [no known file of the paper exists for issues after the end of April].

C. *Saturday Courier. A Family Newspaper—Neutral in Politics and Religion* (Philadelphia weekly edited by Andrew M'Makin).

"New Series" of "Legends of the American Revolution" runs from July 4, 1846, through December 23, 1848.

"George Lippard: His Opponents and the Public"—August 29, 1846.

About Lippard: "Mr. Lippard and His Legends" (by M'Makin)—December 26, 1846.

About Lippard: "Mr. Lippard's Drama" (M'Makin's review of *The Sons of Temperance*)—February 6, 1847.

"Washington and His Generals. The Works of Headley and Lippard"—May 15, 1847.

About Lippard: *"Blanche of Brandywine"* (M'Makin's review of the play based on Lippard's novel by Mrs. H. M. Ward)—May 29, 1847.

Autobiographical preface to reprint of Charles Chauncey Burr's essay on Lippard—January 15, 1848.

D. *Nineteenth Century. A Quarterly Miscellany* (Philadelphia magazine edited by Charles Chauncey Burr).

"The Heart-Broken" (tribute to Charles Brockden Brown). 1848.

"Jesus and the Poor." 1848.

"The Imprisoned Jesus." 1848.

"The Carpenter's Son." 1849.

"Valedictory of the Industrial Congress." 1849.

"The Sisterhood of the Green Veil" (story on the plight of female factory workers). 1849.

E. *Quaker City* (weekly newspaper edited by Lippard)

Attack on the Rev. Alonzo Potter and defense of French novels—December 30, 1848.

"The Gold-Devil: Or, California Now, and A Hundred Years Ago"—January 6, 1849.

"Opinions of the Press" (representative laudatory reviews of Lippard's works from various newspapers)—begins January 6, 1849, and continues through entire run of paper.

"The Quaker City Police Court"—January 13 periodically through August 18, 1849.

Attack on Orestes Brownson—January 13, 1849.

Attack on publishers—January 20, 1849.

Essay on "a National Literature"—February 10, 1849.

"The Dark Sabbath" (one of several "Legends of Every Day" published in the first half of 1849 in the paper)—March 3, 1849.

Attack on "the Iscariot Press"—March 10, 1849.

"The Monster with Three Names"—March 17, 1849.

"The Poor Man" (biblical story)—March 24, 1849.

Comment on James Fenimore Cooper—April 21, 1849.

Attack on plagiarists of *Legends of the American Revolution*—May 5, 1849.

"Twenty-Three Thoughts, by George Lippard"—May 12, 1849.

Article praising early Pennsylvania pietists—May 19, 1849.

Attack on literature as art—June 2, 1849.

Comment on reformist intent of *Quaker City* weekly—June 30, 1849.

"The Tragedy of Grasslinn. A Legend of Northern England"—July 21, 1849.

Brief history of secret societies—August 18, 1849.

Article on Zachary Taylor—August 18, 1849.

Eulogy of Poe—October 20, 1849.

"The Milford Bard" (eulogy of poet John Lofland)—Nevember 3, 1849.

"It Is a Queer World" (account of Poe's last visit)—January 26, 1850.

Review of Lucretia Mott's "Discourse on Woman"—February 9, 1850.

Gloomy letter by Lippard to South Carolina editor Lawrence Badger predicting war between North and South—March 2, 1850.

"Disunion" (more on possible civil war)—March 9, 1850.

"Mass Meeting in the Chinese Museum, in Behalf of the Tailoresses and Other Sewing Women"—March 9, 1850.

Lippard reports attending spiritualist séance—March 23, 1850.

Essay promoting land reform—March 30, 1850.

F. *White Banner.* Volume I. Philadelphia: George Lippard, 1851 (only issue of official organ of the Brotherhood of the Union).

Adonai: The Pilgrim of Eternity.

"Legends of Every Day" (fourteen legends reprinted from *Quaker City* weekly).

"Brotherhood versus Atheistic Sectarianism."

"Editorial Department" (notes on the Brotherhood of the Union and brief literary essays).

"H. F. Constitution of ——— Circle of the Brotherhood of the Union" (sample constitution establishing rules of the Brotherhood).

G. *Sunday Mercury* (Philadelphia newspaper).

"Eleanor; or, Slave Catching in the Quaker City"—January 29 through March 12, 1854.

3. Manuscript Materials

The Historical Society of Pennsylvania. Has file of DuSolle's *Spirit of the Times* and Lippard's *Quaker City* weekly (through 1849), as well as some first editions of Lippard's fiction and microfilms of "A Leaf from Grandfather's Bible" by Sarah Bilbough (Lippard's sister), Lippard's brief diary of the early 1850s, and miscellaneous material relating to the Brotherhood of the Union. The Joseph Jackson Collection contains some sixteen letters in Lippard's hand, a publishing contract for his novel *The Quaker City,* and "Notes on the Brotherhood of the Union."

The Library Company, Philadelphia. Has some early editions of Lippard's work, including *The Killers* and *Thomas Paine, Author-Soldier of the American Revolution.*

The Free Library, Philadelphia. Has the copy of *Eureka* presented by Poe to Lippard, with Lippard's inscription.

Bucks County Historical Society, Pennsylvania. Holds file of the *Citizen Soldier.*

The American Antiquarian Society, Worcester, Massachusetts. Has the most complete file in existence of the *Quaker City* weekly, including all known 1850 issues, plus signed and important editions of much of Lippard's fiction, many of his periodical writings, copies of some of his letters, and certain reviews of his work.

Nearly complete collections of Lippard's fiction are in the Historical Society of Pennsylvania and Library Company, suplemented by the New York Public Library, the Library of Congress, and the Barrett Collection at the University of Virginia. Most of his novels are in the Lyle Wright microfilm series of early American fiction.

SECONDARY SOURCES

1. Bibliographies

Blanck, Jacob (comp.). *Bibliography of American Literature.* IV (New Haven: Yale University Press, 1969). Chronological listing of volumes by Lippard, including first printings, reissues, pirated editions, and certain translations and imitations.

Butterfield, Roger. "A Check List of the Separately Published Works of George Lippard." *Pennsylvania Magazine of History and Biography* 74 (July 1955):302–309. Lists bound Lippard volumes and gives publishing history of certain of his novels.

Jackson, Joseph. "A Bibliography of the Works of George Lippard."
Pennsylvania Magazine of History and Biography 54 (April and October 1930):131–54, 381–83. The first bibliography of Lippard; has since been superseded by Blanck and Butterfield.

2. Books and Parts of Books

Allibone, S. Austin. *A Critical Dictionary of English Literature and American Authors.* Volume II. Philadelphia: J. B. Lippincott and Co., 1858–1871. Contains brief sketch of Lippard.

Bode, Carl, ed. *Anatomy of American Popular Culture, 1840–1861.* Berkeley: University of California Press, 1959. Discusses Lippard's popularity.

[**Bouton, John Bell.**] *The Life and Choice Writings of George Lippard.* New York: H. H. Randall, 1855. A flattering first biography authorized by Lippard. Although romanticized, this is the most useful contemporary account of his life.

Bryan, William A. *George Washington in American Literature.* New York: Columbia University Press, 1952. Mentions the Revolutionary legends in the context of other patriotic fiction.

Clymer, R. Swinburne. *The Book of Rosicruciae.* Quakertown, Penna.: Philosophical Publishing Company, 1947. Misleading argument that Lippard was a Rosicrucian and an ardent abolitionist; reprints some passages from the rare *Adonai: The Pilgrim of Eternity.*

Cowie, Alexander. *The Rise of the American Novel.* New York: American Book Company, 1948. Contains a chapter on the sensationalism and the plots of *The Quaker City.*

Davis, David Brion. *Homicide in American Fiction.* Ithaca, N.Y.: Cornell University Press, 1957. Scattered but suggestive discussion of sex and violence in certain of Lippard's city novels.

Fiedler, Leslie. *Love and Death in the American Novel.* Revised edition. New York: Stein and Day, 1966. Mentions Lippard as prophetic novelist of social protest.

Jackson, Joseph. *Encyclopedia of Philadelphia.* Volume III. Harrisburg: National Historical Association, 1932, pp. 842–45.

———. "George Lippard: Poet of the Proletariat." Ca. 1930. Unpublished and unfinished attempt at a modern biography. Manuscript in the Joseph Jackson Collection, Historical Society of Pennsylvania.

Johnson, Allen, and **Malone, Dumas.** *Dictionary of American Biography.* Volume IX. New York: Charles Scribner's Sons, 1933. Sketch and short bibliography of Lippard by Joseph Jackson.

Kunitz, Stanley J., and Haycraft, Howard, eds. *American Authors, 1600–1900.* New York: H. W. Wilson, 1938. Brief sketch of Lippard.

Mott, Frank Luther. *Golden Multitudes: The Story of Best Sellers in the United States.* New York: Macmillan, 1947. Dismissive passage on *The Quaker City* as "a big, melodramatic humbug."

Noel, Mary. *Villains Galore: The Heyday of the Popular Story Weekly.* New York: Macmillan, 1954. Short discussion of Lippard's serialized fiction in the *Saturday Courier* and the *Quaker City* weekly.

Nye, Russel. *The Unembarrassed Muse: The Popular Arts in America.* New York: Dial, 1970. Brief review of Lippard's sensational urban fiction.

Oberholtzer, Ellis P. *The Literary History of Philadelphia.* Philadelphia: G. W. Jacobs, 1906. About twenty pages on Lippard as a colorful but trashy novelist. Contains some useful biographical information.

Quinn, Arthur Hobson. *Edgar Allan Poe: A Critical Biography.* New York: Appleton-Century, 1941. Mentions Poe's relationship with Lippard.

Reynolds, David S. *Faith in Fiction: The Emergence of Religious Literature in America.* Cambridge, Mass.: Harvard University Press, 1981. Discusses Lippard's religious themes in the context of previous American religious fiction, satirical and affirmative.

Stoehr, Taylor. *Hawthorne's Mad Scientists: Pseudoscience and Social Science in Nineteenth-Century Life and Letters.* Hamden, Conn.: Archon, 1978. Illuminating discussion of such fads as mesmerism, phrenology, homeopathy, and magnetism in popular and major antebellum literature, with passing discussion of Lippard.

Stout, Janis P. *Sodoms in Eden: The City in American Fiction before 1860.* Westport, Conn.: Greenwood Press, 1976. Places Lippard's city novels with Brockden Brown's above merely sensational urban exposés but below the psychological city fiction of Poe and Melville.

Wemyss, Francis Courtney. *Twenty-Six Years of the Life of an Actor and Manager.* New York: Burgess, Stringer, and Co., 1847. Detailed account of the attempted dramatization of *The Quaker City* at the Chesnut Street Theater in 1844.

Ziff, Larzer. *Literary Democracy: The Declaration of Cultural Independence in America.* New York: Viking, 1981. Contains a thoughtful chapter discussing Lippard's sexual and social themes in terms of major literature of the day.

3. Articles

Buhle, Paul. "American Horror," in *Surrealism and Its Popular Accomplices,* ed. Franklin Rosemont (San Francisco: City Lights, 1980). Brief mention of Lippard in the development of American literary horror.

————. "George Lippard and Popular Literary Traditions." *Free Spirits: Annals of the Insurgent Imagination,* no. 2 (San Francisco: City Lights, forthcoming 1983). Relates Lippard's work to the emergence of popular literature, emphasizing his close ties to his workingclass readers.

Butterfield, Roger. "George Lippard and His Secret Brotherhood." *Pennsylvania Magazine of History and Biography* 74 (July 1955):291–309. Spirited review of Lippard's life that focuses on his innovative social views.

Cowie, Alexander. "Monk Hall, Shame of Philadelphia." *New York Times Book Review,* October 22, 1944. Discusses the sensation created by Lippard's most famous novel.

DeGrazia, Emilio. "Edgar Allan Poe, George Lippard, and the Spermaceti and Walnut-Coffin Papers." *Papers of the Bibliographical Society of America* 66 (1972):58–60. Proves that Lippard, not Poe, wrote these literary satires.

————. "Poe's Devoted Democrat, George Lippard." *Poe Studies* 6 (June 1973);6–8. Analyzes Lippard's printed defenses of Poe.

Eaves, Thomas Cary Duncan. "Poe's Last Visit to Philadelphia." *American Literature* 26 (March 1954):44–51. Discusses Lippard's aiding Poe during Poe's visit in July 1849.

Ehrlich, Heyward. "The 'Mysteries' of Philadelphia: Lippard's *Quaker City* and 'Urban' Gothic." *ESQ: A Journal of the American Renaissance* 66 (1st Quarter 1972):50–65. Brief account of the penny-dreadful and *roman-feuilleton* roots of Lippard's fiction, followed by perceptive comparisons between *The Quaker City* and several better-known American novels.

Fiedler, Leslie A. "The Male Novel." *Partisan Review* 37 (1970):74–89. Expanded and reprinted as introduction to Fiedler's edition of *The Monks of Monk Hall* (New York: Odyssey Press, 1970). Lively review of the French and British "city mysteries" genre and of Lippard as a semipornographic novelist who catered mainly to a male audience.

Ford, Henry J. "The Liberty Bell." *American Mercury* 3 (November 1924):279–84. Traces the cherished myth of the ringing of the Liberty Bell on July 4, 1776, to Lippard's legend.

Jablonski, Joseph. "George Lippard and the Rosicrucian Mythos." *Free Spirits: Annals of the Insurgent Imagination,* no. 2 (San Francisco: City Lights, forthcoming 1983). A look at some of the occult and mystical elements in Lippard's work, tracing some of his attitudes to the immigrant German communist-pietists who settled along the Wissahickon Creek in the seventeenth century.

Jackson, Joseph. "George Lippard: Misunderstood Man of Letters." *Pennsylvania Magazine of History and Biography* 54 (October 1930):376–91. Slim review of Lippard's life and fiction.

Pollin, Burton R. "More on Poe and Lippard." *Poe Studies* 7 (June 1974):22–23. Brief account of Lippard's praise of Poe in his columns for the *Citizen Soldier.*

Reynolds, David S. "Lippard, Poe, and the Surrealist Adventure." *Free Spirits: Annals of the Insurgent Imagination,* no. 2 (San Francisco: City Lights, forthcoming 1983). Comparison of surrealist tendencies in Poe's and Lippard's works, focusing on Lippard's use of automatism, black humor, and the erotic.

Ridgely, J. V. "George Lippard's *The Quaker City:* The World of the American Porno-Gothic." *Studies in the Literary Imagination* 7 (Spring 1974):77–94. Close discussion of the plots and racy themes of *The Quaker City.*

Rosemont, Franklin. "George Lippard and the Workers' Movement." *Free Spirits: Annals of the Insurgent Imagination,* no. 2 (San Francisco: City Lights, forthcoming 1983). Focuses on Lippard's role in George Henry Evans's radical land reform movement, his critique of capitalist society, and his association with revolutionaries and trade unionists, especially printers.

———. "Homage to George Lippard." *Free Spirits: Annals of the Insurgent Imagination* no. 2 (San Francisco: City Lights, forthcoming 1983). Brief introduction to Lippard as a precursor of surrealism.

Seecamp, Carsten E. "The Chapter of Perfection: A Neglected Influence on George Lippard." *Pennsylvania Magazine of History and Biography* 94 (April 1970):192–212. Explores Lippard's interest in early Pennsylvania pietists, emphasizing the religious influences on *Paul Ardenheim.*

Siegel, Adrienne. "Brothels, Bets and Bars: Popular Literature as Guidebook to the Urban Underground, 1840–70." *North Dakota*

Quarterly 44 (Spring 1976):5–22. Mentions Lippard in a survey of sensational urban novelists.

Wyld, Lionel D. "George Lippard: Gothicism and Social Consciousness in the Early American Novel." *Four Quarters* 5 (1956):6–12. Discusses *The Quaker City* as prophetic of later urban fiction.

4. Dissertations

DeGrazia, Emilio. "The Life and Works of George Lippard." Ph.D. dissertation, Ohio State University, 1969. Thorough chronological discussion of Lippard's life and works that argues that Lippard had four controlling "dreams": the grotesque, social and political reform, intense patriotism, and nonsectarian Christianity.

Thomas, Dwight Rembert. "Poe in Philadelphia, 1838–1844: A Documentary Record." Ph.D. Dissertation, University of Pennsylvania, 1978. Reprints and analyzes excerpts from Lippard's literary columns in the *Spirit of the Times* and the *Citizen Soldier*.

Index